OECD
Economic Surveys

Netherlands

2006

OECD

ORGANISATION FOR ECONOMIC CO-OPERATION AND DEVELOPMENT

ORGANISATION FOR ECONOMIC CO-OPERATION AND DEVELOPMENT

The OECD is a unique forum where the governments of 30 democracies work together to address the economic, social and environmental challenges of globalisation. The OECD is also at the forefront of efforts to understand and to help governments respond to new developments and concerns, such as corporate governance, the information economy and the challenges of an ageing population. The Organisation provides a setting where governments can compare policy experiences, seek answers to common problems, identify good practice and work to co-ordinate domestic and international policies.

The OECD member countries are: Australia, Austria, Belgium, Canada, the Czech Republic, Denmark, Finland, France, Germany, Greece, Hungary, Iceland, Ireland, Italy, Japan, Korea, Luxembourg, Mexico, the Netherlands, New Zealand, Norway, Poland, Portugal, the Slovak Republic, Spain, Sweden, Switzerland, Turkey, the United Kingdom and the United States. The Commission of the European Communities takes part in the work of the OECD.

OECD Publishing disseminates widely the results of the Organisation's statistics gathering and research on economic, social and environmental issues, as well as the conventions, guidelines and standards agreed by its members.

> *This survey is published on the responsibility of the Economic and Development Review Committee of the OECD, which is charged with the examination of the economic situation of member countries.*

Publié également en français

Table of contents

Figures

BASIC STATISTICS OF THE NETHERLANDS (2004)

THE LAND

Area (1 000 km^2):		Major cities, 1st January 2004 (thousand inhabitants):	
Total	42	Amsterdam	739
Agricultural land	23	Rotterdam	599
Woodland	4	The Hague	469

THE PEOPLE

Population (thousands)	16 258	Employment (thousands, full-time equivalents):	
Number of inhabitants per km^2 of land	481	Total	6 454
Net natural increase (thousands)	52	Agriculture, fishing and forestry	218
		Industry	859
		Construction	436
		Other activities	4 941

PRODUCTION

Gross domestic product, 2004 (million euros)	488 642	Gross fixed investment:	
GDP per head (EUR)	30 055	Per cent of GDP	19
		Per head (EUR)	5 821

THE PUBLIC SECTOR

Per cent of GDP:		Composition of Parliament (number of seats):	
Public consumption	24	Christian democratic appeal	44
Current receipts	44	Labour Party (PvdA)	42
Current disbursements	51	Popular Party for freedom and democracy	27
		Socialist Party	8
		List Pim Fortuyn	7
		Other	22
		Total	150
		Last general election	January 2003

FOREIGN TRADE

Exports of goods and services (% of GDP)	67	Imports of goods and services (% of GDP)	60

THE CURRENCY

Monetary unit	Euro	Currency units per US$, average of daily figures:	
		Year 2004	0.80
		November 2005	0.85

Note: An international comparison of certain basic statistics is given in an annex table.

Executive summary

After five years of sluggishness, an economic recovery finally appears in the offing in the Netherlands. The financial imbalances that contributed to the downturn at the start of the decade have been corrected, thanks to well-tailored policies for the most part, and exports have already rebounded. The severity of the downturn – the output gap stands at –3% in 2005 – partly reflects an unusual succession of adverse shocks. Even so, other OECD economies have rebounded more quickly in similar conditions, suggesting an intrinsic difficulty to return to trend – a lack of resilience. The present Survey examines why the Netherlands lacks resilience and what could be done to avoid the recurrence of such difficulties. It also reviews how the re-emergence of large fiscal imbalances could be avoided, while making progress towards sustainability in a context of population ageing. As well, the Survey examines what could be done to raise trend growth through a combination of higher labour utilisation and stronger productivity growth.

Increasing resilience. Like several other European countries, the Dutch economy is slow to return to trend. Traditional re-equilibrating forces appear weak, notably the reaction of unit labour costs to slack, thus holding up these costs, eroding international competitiveness and limiting the extent to which inflation falls. One of the reasons for such behaviour of unit labour costs is that firms face obstacles to adjust employment to bring down these costs. To improve the economy's capacity to return to trend quickly, future reforms should further reduce the strictness of EPL.

Putting public finances on a sustainable path. Following the large deterioration in public finances over 2000-03, consolidation measures have successfully cut the budget deficit to 1.6% of GDP in 2005. Continued efforts at consolidation will be needed over the next few years so as to achieve a sustainable fiscal position. The present fiscal rule (ceilings on public spending over the legislature) is appropriate, but could be strengthened to avoid that cyclical and unexpected revenue windfalls are spent. The amount of tax expenditures and the practice of earmarking natural gas revenues to special projects will be reviewed.

Increasing labour utilisation. The Netherlands has initiated a very substantial programme of reforms of its labour market and social security institutions, including health care. These reforms will shift people from social benefit dependence into employment and contribute to structural growth and budget consolidation. In the future, more needs to be done to reduce incentives for early retirement. This would entail monitoring access to publicly subsidised routes to early retirement and indexing the future official retirement age to life expectancy. To ease the trade-off between women's participation in the labour force and family responsibilities, marginal effective tax rates should be lowered further, possibly by reducing further the taper rate at which childcare subsidies are progressively withdrawn as household income rises.

Removing barriers to competition and enhancing innovation activity to raise productivity growth. The Netherlands has not experienced the surge in productivity growth observed outside the European Union, particularly in retail and financial services. To do so, it will be necessary to go further in removing barriers to competition in these key ICT-using service sectors and in further eliminating disincentives to entrepreneurship. Innovation activity (the subject of the in-depth *chapter) will benefit from the reforms in framework conditions (e.g., creating an attractive business climate) and tertiary education, as well as from the rationalisation of the various forms of government support to innovation, all of which will make the Netherlands more attractive for both domestic and inward R&D spending.*

ISBN 92-64-03669-5
OECD Economic Surveys: Netherlands
© OECD 2006

Assessment and recommendations

The economy is recovering; even so, improving resilience, public finances and potential growth remain key challenges

After having stagnated during the past five years, the Dutch economy finally appears to have begun to recover. Substantial progress has been made towards correcting the financial imbalances that contributed to the downturn. Furthermore, major labour market, social benefit and health care reforms are underway to enhance labour utilisation and labour productivity. At the same time, cost competitiveness is being gradually restored. Barring further international energy price spikes, the Dutch economy should grow above trend in 2006, turning the page on one of the worst periods of stagnation since the 1930s. Even so, the economy remains vulnerable in the face of adverse shocks.

- While several special factors have exacerbated the recent stagnation, the five years it has taken for the economy to begin to recover suggests a lack of resilience (Chapter 1).

- The prolonged downturn has taken its toll on public finances, necessitating substantial consolidation measures since 2003 to respect the Stability and Growth Pact, but more needs to be done to achieve a sustainable path (Chapter 2).

- There is scope to limit the amount of additional budget consolidation by implementing structural reforms that would further increase labour utilisation (Chapter 3) and productivity growth (Chapter 4).

- Enhancing the diffusion of innovation would also contribute to faster trend growth (Chapter 5).

The economy has been mired in a long downturn, but a recovery is in the offing for 2006

Dutch economic growth has been weak since the start of the decade. A temporary rebound in economic activity unfolded in 2004, but was stalled by weak domestic and external demand, not least due to rising oil prices. After five years of below trend growth, the output gap has fallen from a peak of +4% in 2000 (compared with +2% for the euro area) to –3% in 2005 (–2% for the euro area), making this a very ample cycle by both historical and international comparison. The magnitude of the downturn is partly explained by the fact that a number of factors that boosted growth in the late 1990s – notably developments in housing and stock markets and in the euro-dollar exchange rate – have since contributed less (housing) or even dragged the economy down. In addition, the decline in capital market returns adversely affected pension funds, necessitating large increases in pension contribution rates to restore solvency. These increases are estimated to have reduced GDP by 2 percentage points. The impact of these factors was aggravated by a large loss of international cost competitiveness, even against other euro area countries.

Competitiveness is now improving and exports are once again stimulating the economy. The fiscal and pension fund financial imbalances have been largely corrected. Corporate earnings are growing fast, helping build up business capital formation. Real GDP accelerated sharply in the second quarter and unemployment declined slightly during the summer, after having stabilised during the first half of the year. Assuming that oil prices stabilise and that there is a pick up in other European economies, strengthening exports and domestic demand could well propel annual economic growth to above 2% in 2006.

Reforms to increase labour-market flexibility are important for fostering macroeconomic resilience

While special factors have undoubtedly exacerbated the recent downswing, the slow speed at which the economy is returning to trend suggests that re-equilibrating forces are weak. Empirical evidence presented in this *Survey* shows that inflation is slow to respond to cyclical conditions, especially in comparison with non-EU countries. This appears to be so because adjustment channels have operated weakly, notably the response of labour costs to cyclical downturns. As firms have difficulty adjusting their levels of employment owing to employment protection legislation (EPL) for regular contracts, which is strict by international comparison, labour productivity growth falls sharply during the initial stages of an economic downturn, holding up unit labour costs, and therefore eroding international competitiveness and limiting the extent to which inflation falls. Even though there is a reasonable degree of wage moderation when there is labour market slack, this occurs only after a significant lag. In the latest cycle, labour hoarding was unusually large because many employees recruited during the economic boom of the late 1990s had permanent contracts, employers had faced high hiring costs and they had initially anticipated a quick recovery. Also, labour costs were inflated by large increases in pension premiums. All of this suggests that the adjustment of unit labour costs has occurred only slowly in the face of economic slack, thus lengthening the period of stagnation required for market forces to operate. On the whole, the slowness of adjustment appears to result, for the most part, from the strictness of EPL on regular contracts, which increases employment adjustment costs.

The government has announced measures to ease EPL, which come into effect in October 2006, and the Social and Economic Council will advise on further reforms. The announced measures lower the administrative costs of dismissals and increase flexibility for employers. Even so, EPL will remain strict by international comparison. In this context:

● The government should go further in easing EPL on regular contracts by reducing the procedural inconveniences for dismissing a worker and widening the circumstances in which a dismissal is justified.

Fiscal consolidation is needed to put public finances on a sustainable path in a context of population ageing

After the sharp deterioration of public finances in 2002-03, consolidation measures have been implemented to cut the general government deficit. While the deficit has been reduced to 1.6% of GDP in 2005, fiscal consolidation has had an adverse impact on short-term economic growth. With hindsight, fiscal policy was too loose during the upswing, allowing a marked deterioration of the structural deficit that did not leave enough room for automatic stabilisers to work fully during the subsequent downturn while adhering to the Stability and Growth Pact.

After several years of consolidation, the structural deficit is likely to approach 0.5% of GDP in 2005. While this is an impressive achievement by EU standards, the evolution of public finances nonetheless raises a number of concerns. With economic growth projected to rise above trend and with large expected windfalls in natural gas revenues, the government has sought to restore part of the additional tax burden imposed on households in recent years and to invest in structural reforms, for example by increasing outlays for child care. As a result, the deficit is projected to rise to 1.8% of GDP in 2006, implying some deterioration in the structural deficit. This development shifts public finances further away from the sustainable path that was estimated by the authorities in 2000 to require a surplus of 1% of GDP, on what turned out to be optimistic assumptions, leaving a challenge for 2006 (using windfalls for further deficit reduction) and beyond. In the longer run a more ambitious fiscal strategy seems warranted:

- The opportunity of economic recovery should be used to undertake a new medium-term consolidation programme that moves public finances towards a sustainable path – a level that will soon be re-estimated by the Netherlands Bureau for Economic Policy Analysis (CPB) – while at the same time strengthening medium-term growth prospects.

The fiscal framework has many merits, but the expenditure ceilings tend to be circumvented by recourse to tax expenditures. These tax expenditures should therefore be reviewed. The earmarking of natural gas revenues to special programmes should also be subject to close examination. It is vital that these revenues be used for capital expenditures, not current expenditures. This is in accordance with the operating rules of the fund (Fund for the improvement of the structure of the economy, FES) into which gas revenues are paid. Moreover, the authorities should ensure that investments made with these resources earn adequate rates of return, thereby enabling both current and future generations to profit fully and equitably from the natural resource rents. A study group is evaluating both the fiscal framework and the system of spending gas revenues via the FES and will report in 2006. This advice will be used by the next administration to determine the future of FES.

Achieving a sustainable medium-term path for public finances would be facilitated by increases in the retirement age. Rising life expectancy at retirement age is substantially increasing pension costs. At the same time, the health status of people at the official retirement age (65-years old) is now better than in the past – most people are healthy enough at this age to continue working.

- The government should consider indexing the future official retirement age to life expectancy and encourage social partners to make concomitant adjustments to the age at which (actuarially fair) early retirement can be taken in occupational pension schemes, so as to lessen the impact of rising life expectancy on pension costs and support potential growth.

Reforms to tighten eligibility to social benefits will contribute to the needed budget consolidation and raise labour utilisation

Budget consolidation will also benefit from the measures that have been implemented or are in the pipeline to shift people from dependence on social benefits into employment. Disability benefit recipients aged less than 50 are being re-tested for eligibility and incentives for the partially disabled to use their residual work capacity are being strengthened. The reform of social assistance in 2004, which decentralised this programme to municipalities and gave them strong incentives to encourage the return to work of social assistance beneficiaries, also goes in the right direction. As well, the government plans to reform unemployment benefits (UB) by reducing maximum benefit duration from 5 years to 38 months, which nonetheless remains long by international comparison, and by making duration more dependent on the employment record and less on age. On the other hand, the government has introduced a new welfare-level benefit for older unemployed persons which, in contrast to social assistance, is not subject to an assets – means test for people aged 50 or over nor to a partner income test for people aged 60 or over. The scheme is subject to a sunset clause and will be evaluated in 2010.

- The impact of the reform of the UB-scheme on its use as an exit-route to early retirement should be closely monitored. Even after the reform, the maximum duration of the benefit is relatively long compared with other countries, where duration of 1-2 years is more usual.

- The plans to dispense older persons with care responsibilities from job search obligations may be a cost-effective way to address the increase in long-term care needs, but should be monitored to avoid abuse.

Other social benefit reforms will help reduce unemployment and poverty traps and raise work incentives

The Dutch authorities have reduced unemployment and poverty traps in recent years. A notable exception concerns sole earner households with children earning a modal income, as they gradually lose a tax credit when their income increases. The government has rightly decided to integrate the various tax credits for people with children in 2006 and progressively withdraw the tax credits from the modal income at a taper rate of 6%.

- The government should see whether further action is feasible to reduce unemployment traps by examining further the trade-off between increasing in-work benefits, so as to reduce remaining traps, against the adverse effects on labour supply further up the income scale.

Work incentives for older workers are increasing thanks to the reform of early retirement schemes

The reforms to shift some people off social benefits and into employment should help to increase the employment rate for older workers (45%), which is below the OECD average (50%). In this regard, the recent reforms of disability benefits, unemployment benefits and social assistance are important. These changes complement the termination of tax subsidies for early retirement schemes from the beginning of 2006. However, a new (tax-favoured) life-course-savings scheme offering opportunities to take leave that should help workers to cope with their family responsibilities and to invest in training, potentially prolonging working lives, can also be used as an individual early retirement scheme.

- The government should monitor the use of the new individual life-course-savings scheme and prevent it from becoming an alternative route to early retirement.

Incentives are needed to increase working time –
the shortest in the OECD – especially for women

Even though employment rates are relatively high, labour utilisation is held back by the shortest annual working time in the OECD (1 357 hours in 2004). An important factor reducing average working time is the high proportion of women working part time. Many women have chosen to work part-time because of the high cost of suitable childcare, school hours that are ill adapted to the needs of working parents (many schools send children home at lunchtime and on Wednesday afternoons) and the absence of affordable pre- and after-school facilities. A new Childcare Law was implemented in January 2005 that aims at making it easier for parents (in practice, mothers) to reconcile family responsibilities and work. The government pays a subsidy that on average amounts to $\frac{1}{3}$ of childcare costs. Employers are on average expected to pay a further one-third, with the remainder to be paid by parents. The government subsidies are means tested, which enables a larger subsidy to be paid at lower incomes out of a given budget but increases marginal effective tax rates at higher incomes. The government recently increased the budget for childcare subsidies by € 130 million to reduce the taper rate at which its subsidy is withdrawn as household income rises, making childcare more affordable for middle-income households. The employers' contribution to child care will be monitored in 2006. The government also rightly increased the budget for lunchtime and after-school care facilities by € 70 million, which appears to be particularly cost effective for increasing female working time. More could be done to increase working time by making it easier for parents with youngsters to reconcile family and work life:

- Notwithstanding the 2006 evaluation, the government should consider further reducing the taper rate for withdrawing childcare subsidies as household income rises. The government is rightly considering increasing its support for "out-of-school hours care", so that mothers can work longer hours. Furthermore, schools should be required to make arrangements so that children are not sent home when teachers are absent.

- To increase incentives to work more hours, marginal effective tax rates should be reduced. Budget room for such reductions could be found by broadening the income tax base. An option could be to further limit tax deductions for mortgage interest payments on owner-occupied housing; the government already has taken some steps in this regard (for example, for owner-occupiers moving house, tax deductibility is limited to interest on that part of the mortgage that is equal to the home's purchase price less equity realised from the sale of the previous home).

*Social partners should remove obstacles to longer
working time*

The short duration of working time in the Netherlands, like in other European countries, can be explained partly by the activities of trade unions, which have tried to cushion employment losses through lower number of hours worked per employee. Now that the government has dropped the distinctions in regulations between overtime and normal working time on the one hand, and standard and agreed time on the other, in favour of a maximum duration of 48 hours per week averaged over a period of 13 weeks (as stipulated in the EU working time directive), only collective agreements stand in the way of extending working time if employers and employees find that mutually advantageous.

- Social partners should review the existing working time clauses in collective agreements, inasmuch as they reduce labour utilisation and lower income per capita, with a view to phasing out existing obstacles (notably, high overtime premiums) for individual employees wishing to work longer hours to earn more, doing so.

*Increasing competition in product markets would
boost productivity growth*

Even though the level of Dutch productivity is high, its growth has trended down. This differs from the evolution in some other countries, such as the United States and Australia, where productivity growth has accelerated since the mid-1990s. Sluggish productivity growth is often associated with a lack of product market competition, as firms protected from competitive pressures have less incentive to increase their efficiency. According to the product market regulation (PMR) indicator, the Netherlands occupies an intermediate position. However, it has relatively high barriers to entrepreneurship, reflecting complex, time-consuming and expensive procedures to obtain licences and permits. Moreover, personal costs of bankruptcy are high, which is likely to discourage entry and growth of firms. Against this backdrop, the authorities have embarked on a medium-term plan aimed at alleviating the burden of regulation. They are right to envisage reducing the personal costs of bankruptcy by offering the bankrupt individual a "clean slate" by way of discharge. They also rightly plan a simplification of the licence and permits system by introducing a "silence is consent" rule.

With respect to corporate governance, the government has decided to increase the power of shareholders. The practice of co-optation (in which existing members of the supervisory board select the new members) was abolished along with non-voting shares with the introduction of the new structural regime. Co-optation and certification (trust offices that are on friendly terms with the management hold the shares and issue non-voting certificates) in the past have discouraged hostile takeovers.

*Less strict regulation of the distribution sector
could boost productivity growth*

In countries where productivity has accelerated in recent years, much of the increase has taken place in two key ICT-using service sectors – distribution and financial services. In the Netherlands, the development of large retail stores with a high use of ICT has been hindered by strict zoning regulations and regulation of shop opening hours, inhibiting the exploitation of economies of scale. The liberalisation of shop opening hours is to be evaluated next year. Municipalities have a large influence on the location of (large) outlets due to their responsibility in drawing up zoning plans but have weak incentives to authorise the establishment of such outlets and might be inclined to favour insiders. In the financial sector, the main barrier to greater use of ICT to raise productivity growth is the lack of integration of retail banking across Europe.

- The Netherlands should consider further liberalising shop opening hours, monitor the land-use policies of municipalities and give them greater incentives to authorise the entry of large outlets.

- To remove barriers to integration in retail financial services, the Dutch authorities and their European counterparts should fully implement the Financial Services Action Plan and apply the four-level "Lamfalussy framework".

Reforms in framework conditions are needed to spur innovation activity

Knowledge creation in the Netherlands is strong – scientific publications per capita are the sixth highest in the OECD and the citation impact is high – but innovation activity is only around the average for OECD countries according to the EIS Summary Innovation Index, undermining productivity growth. This combination of strong knowledge creation but only average innovation activity is characterised as the Dutch paradox. The authorities have started to address this weakness. They have established the "Innovation Platform" – a high-level group of government, business and academic leaders – in charge of formulating new policy initiatives. A number of reforms specific to innovation policy would help in this respect, as discussed below, but framework conditions could also make an important contribution to spurring innovation activity. The relatively limited number of enterprises undertaking non-technological innovations, process innovations, and introducing products that are new to the firm suggests that incentives to innovate are lacking. Increasing entrepreneurship and product market competition, and making social institutions more innovation friendly, would help to strengthen this aspect of innovation activity. While product market regulation limits competition and the entry rate of firms is average, there is much less experimentation than in the United States and fewer exits, undermining innovation activity. Moreover, surveys of social attitudes point to a culture that does not favour risk taking and the pursuit of excellence. The government is trying to change these attitudes through education programmes. Likewise, as noted, it is reforming bankruptcy law to reduce the personal costs of bankruptcy and increase the options for a quick re-start of non-fraudulent bankrupts. There are also other options that could be considered:

- Further easing strict EPL on regular contracts, as recommended above to enhance resilience, would also support innovation by facilitating work re-organisation, especially in industries implementing radical innovation.

- Similarly, lowering barriers to entrepreneurship, as recommended above to increase product market competition, would increase pressure to implement radical innovations.

The Netherlands should be more attractive for private R&D

One of the most important innovation indicators, business R&D intensity, is relatively weak in the Netherlands, at 1% of GDP compared with an OECD average of 1.5%. About 60% of the shortfall in the business R&D intensity relative to the OECD average is linked to the specialisation of the Dutch economy in R&D extensive sectors. The remaining 40% can be explained by a number of factors among which, low R&D inflows adjusted for the openness of the economy. A key factor in making the R&D climate more attractive is to increase the supply of scientists and engineers.

- The government has recently reformed immigration laws to facilitate entry of knowledge workers but should go further by introducing a points system, as in other countries.

- Dutch universities should also be encouraged to compete more aggressively for foreign science and engineering students.

- Work permit rules should be relaxed to make it easier for foreign students to stay in the Netherlands after graduation.

The government aims to strengthen linkages between public research organisations (PRO) (many of which are specifically designed to create knowledge and transfer it to firms) and firms in order to increase (domestic as well as inward) private R&D. In a recent initiative to strengthen such linkages, the government introduced a system of innovation vouchers that can be used by small and medium-sized enterprises to buy knowledge from (semi-) public knowledge institutes (enhancing demand driven research). The government has also rationalised its financial support for R&D activity, which used to be dispersed among a variety of agencies with different objectives, so as to improve co-ordination. Finally, government has introduced an arrangement (Regional Action and Attention for Knowledge innovation) to strengthen the relationship between higher (vocational) education and the SMEs.

- The government should continue to strengthen the linkages between firms and knowledge institutes to enhance the use of (scientific) knowledge in new products, processes and services thereby helping to solve the Dutch paradox of strong knowledge creation combined with low levels of commercialisation.

- Linkages between public knowledge institutes and private firms could be strengthened by making university funding partly dependent on performance in diffusion of knowledge to firms.

- Flexibility in university pay scales should be more widely used to increase incentives for researchers to co-operate with firms.

Tertiary education should be made more attractive

Another key innovation indicator that is relatively weak in the Netherlands is the proportion of the population with tertiary education, which is below the middle ranking of the OECD countries included in the EIS Summary Innovation Index. This ranking is likely to deteriorate as the extent to which the proportion of the population with such attainment in the younger age group (aged 25-34) exceeds that in the older age group (35-54) is less than in most other countries. Low attainment in the younger age group is largely explained by the absence of differentiation in the supply of tertiary education. While enrolment of students in tertiary A (mainly theoretical programmes preparing for research and high-skill professions) programmes is at about the OECD average, the absence of shorter (two or three years) tertiary vocational programmes explains low enrolment in vocational programmes and brings down total average enrolment. The low degree of differentiation in the supply of tertiary education is also evident from fixed tuition fees, relatively long duration of programmes and high barriers to entry for new suppliers of higher education. Therefore:

- The government should encourage universities to offer short (two-year) courses, as are available in most other countries.

- The authorities should differentiate tuition fees, as this will provide universities with an incentive to offer courses that are more attractive to students. Furthermore, the authorities should continue their experiments allowing more private education suppliers to compete for public education funds so as to enhance the quality and diversity of courses offered.

ISBN 92-64-03669-5
OECD Economic Surveys: Netherlands
© OECD 2006

Chapter 1

Challenges faced by the Dutch economy

The Dutch economy is finally recovering, after having stagnated since the start of the decade. This first part of this chapter analyses the forces that are driving the present recovery, notably the progress made towards correcting the imbalances that caused the stagnation. It then discusses, based on detailed empirical evidence, why it took longer to return to trend growth in the Netherlands than in some other OECD countries – in other words, why the Dutch economy lacks resilience. The second part of this chapter gives an overview of medium-term challenges that will become increasingly important in the future: how to make the path of public finances sustainable in a context of population ageing; how to better utilise potential labour resources; how to boost productivity growth, in particular in the services sectors; and how to stimulate innovation activity so as to boost potential output growth.

Short-term prospects

The Dutch economy finally appears ready to recover, turning the page on one of the worst periods of sluggishness in recent decades. After having been a rising star during the second half of the 1990s – with annual growth rates hovering around 4% – the economy sharply decelerated at the start of the decade and then remained mired in stagnation (Table 1.1). The negative forces that weighed on growth during the past five years are now

Table 1.1. **Netherlands: demand, output and prices**[1]

| | 2001 | 2002 | 2003 | 2004 | Projections | | |
					2005	2006	2007
	Percentage changes						
Demand and output (volume)							
Private consumption[2]	1.4	0.9	−0.7	0.0	0.2	−1.7 (1.6)	2.0
Government consumption[2]	4.8	3.3	2.4	0.0	−0.6	7.3 (1.3)	1.5
Gross fixed capital formation	0.2	−4.5	−3.5	2.9	1.4	3.3	2.1
Private sector residential	2.0	−6.5	−3.2	6.3	5.9	1.2	1.5
Private sector non-residential	−2.9	−7.6	−4.0	4.2	−0.9	6.2	3.4
Public sector	9.7	10.2	−2.8	−6.2	1.2	−2.3	−1.3
Final domestic demand	1.9	0.3	−0.5	0.6	0.3	1.7	1.9
Change in stockbuilding[3]	−0.8	−0.6	0.2	0.2	−0.4	−0.1	0.0
Total domestic demand	1.0	−0.4	−0.3	0.8	−0.2	1.5	1.9
Exports of goods and services	1.6	0.9	2.0	8.5	4.3	6.1	6.4
Imports of goods and services	2.2	0.3	2.0	7.8	3.6	5.6	6.0
Change in net exports[3]	−0.3	0.5	0.1	0.9	0.7	0.9	0.8
GDP at market prices	1.4	0.1	−0.1	1.7	0.7	2.2	2.5
Inflation							
GDP deflator	5.2	3.8	2.5	0.9	1.5	2.0	1.6
Private consumption deflator	4.6	3.0	2.2	1.1	1.1	1.5	1.0
Harmonised index of consumer price	5.1	3.9	2.2	1.4	1.5	1.7	0.8
	In per cent						
Others							
General Government financial balance[4]	−0.3	−2.0	−3.2	−2.1	−1.6	−1.8	−1.5
Unemployment rate	2.5	2.9	4.0	4.9	6.2	5.9	5.0
Household saving ratio[5]	4.6	5.2	5.2	7.3	6.0	7.0	7.1
Current account balance[4]	2.4	2.9	2.8	3.3	5.8	6.8	8.0
Short-term interest rates	4.3	3.3	2.3	2.1	2.2	2.2	2.9
Long-term interest rates	5.0	4.9	4.1	4.1	3.4	3.7	4.1

1. National accounts are based on official chain-linked data. This introduces a discrepancy in the identity between real demand components and GDP. For further details see *OECD Economic Outlook*, Sources and Methods, (*www.oecd.org/eco/sources-and-methods*).
2. Numbers in brackets are adjusted for the new compulsory health care system to be implemented in 2006 which will replace the partly private system; private health care expenditure will become public expenditure.
3. Contributions to changes in real GDP (percentage of real GDP in previous year).
4. As a percentage of GDP.
5. As a percentage of disposable income, including savings in life insurance and pension schemes.
Source: OECD Economic Outlook 78 database.

dissipating and domestic demand should soon become more dynamic. Nonetheless, the Netherlands will probably continue to lack resilience in the face of shocks: empirical evidence discussed in this chapter shows that re-equilibrating forces operate weakly, hindering the reactivity of the economy when demand imbalances accumulate. Reforms to reinforce the economy's responsiveness would go a long way towards securing more stable economic growth in the future.

What caused the stagnation?

The period of below-trend growth that started in 2001 has been long and severe. After the brisk expansion during the second half of the 1990s, signs of overheating appeared at the turn of the century, when the output gap is estimated to have reached about 4% of GDP and unemployment fell close to 2½ per cent – below the estimated NAIRU. As the world economy stalled and stock markets plunged, Dutch growth decelerated sharply and fell below trend. There was a temporary pickup in 2004, as private consumption expenditure stabilised, following the contraction of the year before, and exports benefited from the strong demand in non-euro area partner countries and fixed investment gathered strength. However, the recovery faltered by the end of 2004 (as in the entire euro area), further extending the period of sluggishness and increasing the output gap to the estimated level of –3% of GDP in 2005, which is unusually large by historical and international standards. The labour market has remained weak in this environment, with the standardised unemployment rate having reached 4.8% during the first half of the year.

External factors made an important contribution to the downturn. Being a very open economy, the Netherlands was highly exposed to the downturn in world trade in the early part of the decade and then suffered from the prolonged weakness of the euro area. As well, the hefty increases in real wages at the end of the past decade reduced competitiveness and weighed on international market shares. Estimates of Dutch world market shares (adjusted for re-exports) suggest they have declined since the start of the decade, partly due to the strong value of the euro against other currencies and the progressive integration of emerging economies (notably China) in global trade, but also to the unfavourable evolution of unit labour costs relative to other euro area countries. Even though net foreign trade did not make a negative contribution to growth, it stopped making the strong contribution to growth recorded in the past decade.

As well, domestic factors played a significant role in the stagnation. As in many other OECD countries, business capital formation fell at the turn of the century, as Dutch firms tried to reduce indebtedness and focussed on restoring profits after the investment surge of the late 1990s. While business investment made a recovery in 2004, private consumption remained in the doldrums. After having been the main force propelling the end-of-century expansion, private consumption has remained stagnant during the last five years – even declining in real terms in 2003 and perhaps in 2005 – despite declining private savings rates as Dutch consumers have reacted to the deterioration of their economic and financial environments by scaling back their spending.

This pattern of private consumption diverged from that in the United Kingdom and United States, where it stayed firm and helped the economy recover from its downturn. This divergence occurred despite households having common features in the three countries, such as an inclination to cash in on housing equity to finance consumption spending, a willingness to contract large debts to purchase houses and an appetite for accumulating large pension wealth in the form of fully-funded pension schemes. US and UK households followed a pattern of "consumption smoothing" – reducing their saving rates in slow times so as to maintain their life-time consumption path – Although Dutch households also smoothed their consumption pattern to some extent, several factors appear to have contributed to the meagre growth of private consumption expenditures:

- Household real disposable income was hit more severely in The Netherlands than in the other two countries due to the wage moderation agreements between social partners, increases in taxes and in health care and pension fund contributions, employment losses and significant declines in property income.

- Unlike the continuous increase of house prices over the recent past in the United Kingdom and the United States, house price increases slowed considerably in the Netherlands after 2001 and did not provide a cushion for the decline in stock market prices. As a result, Dutch household were hit more permanently by the collapse of equity prices, with their net financial wealth falling from a peak of 225% of GDP in 1999 (including pension fund assets) to 167% of GDP in 2003 (DNB, 2004, DNB, 2005) – significantly weighing down private consumption.

- As well, household indebtedness has risen in the Netherlands to levels unseen in most other OECD countries. Indeed, the amount of outstanding loans contracted by households jumped from 63% of GDP in 1995 to 104% of GDP in 2003, well beyond the rise observed in the UK and the US (DNB, 2005). With financial wealth on the decline, the balance sheets of households came under stress, in particular for families having contracted large mortgage loans to finance their first accession to property and for those who had cashed in on their housing wealth to finance current spending or buy equities Households have reacted to the drop in stock markets in 2001 and 2002 by shifting to safer assets (*e.g.*, saving deposits) and by starting to repay debts. The balance sheet restructuring is now well underway and, according to preliminary estimates from the Dutch National Bank Household Survey, the average amount of debt per household fell from € 52 395 in 2004 per household to € 48 020 in 2005. Even so, Dutch households remain highly indebted by international standards, posing an obvious risk to the outlook in case of a significant increase in interest rates and/or sharp drop in house prices, which may yet occur. This is notably the case for certain income groups, including low-income families having acceded to house ownership, who could see their net wealth turn negative if house prices were to decline by 20% or so (DNB, 2004).

The protracted period of below-trend growth and the accumulation of slack has put inflation under downward pressure and helped to regain control of wage and production cost increases. Despite rising energy prices, headline harmonised inflation decelerated to 1.6% in August 2005, one of the lowest in the euro area, with core inflation decelerating even further to 0.8% in mid-2005. Contractual nominal wage growth in the market sector is estimated to fall to 0.6% in 2005, down from 4.2% in 2001, helping to restore profitability and improve competitiveness.

Outlook for 2006

The improvement in households' balance sheets and the decline in inflation and wage pressures bode well for the economic recovery. Indeed, there are signs that some growth momentum is finally building up. Real GDP sharply accelerated in the second quarter of 2005 and unemployment slightly declined during the summer. With growth expected to remain strong in the global economy, improved cost competitiveness, a pause in fiscal consolidation planned in the short-term and a gradual resolution of pension fund imbalances, the Dutch economy is finally gathering some speed and is likely to expand at slightly above the trend rate in 2006. Exports will continue to be the driving force, thanks to robust world trade growth and an improvement in relative unit labour costs. Better sales prospects will improve companies' financial situation along with an increase in capacity utilisation, so that business investment should gradually gain strength and employment start growing at a faster pace in 2006. The turnaround in employment is supported by recent reforms increasing labour supply, which will also raise the unemployment rate temporarily in the current year, after which it is projected to fall in 2006. With real house prices apparently still increasing at a moderately positive rate and households further improving their balance sheets, growth in private consumption is expected to exceed that in real disposable income in 2006.

Monetary conditions on the other hand, still appear to be too tight for the Netherlands based on Taylor rule calculations (Figure 1.1). The conjunction of low inflation and an unusually large output gap would imply, according to a Taylor rule, a lower short-term interest rate than currently. The European Central Bank sets interest rates for the entire euro area, with the obvious consequence that they may not always be adapted for a particular country. This underscores the importance of economic responsiveness in the wake of a negative shock and of conducting adequate fiscal policy.

Figure 1.1. **Euro short term interest rate and Taylor rule for the Netherlands**[1]

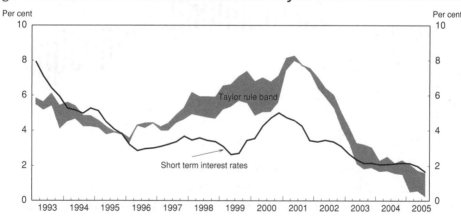

1. The Taylor rule was calculated as i = 2% + CORE + (w1 * GAP) + (w2 * CPI_DEV) where CORE is the year-on year change of core consumer price inflation, GAP is the output gap and CPI_DEV is the deviation of headline consumer price inflation from an annual inflation target set at 1.75%. The weights w1 and w2 are allowed to vary between 0.3 and 0.7 and the chart shows the minimum and the maximum of the range.
Source: OECD Outlook 78 Database and Secretariat estimates.

Medium-term challenges

While a short-term economic rebound may be in the offing, this will not resolve the medium-term challenges faced by the Netherlands. Improving the responsiveness of the Dutch economy in the aftermath of shocks, so as to return more promptly to trend and avoid the stagnation of the past five years, would address a long-lasting weakness. Bringing public finances on a sustainable path, in the context of population ageing, is also a long-term challenge. This would be made all the more easier with increased potential growth. To this end, there is a substantial reserve of untapped labour potential that can be mobilised, residing notably in a different split between working and leisure times over the lifespan. Boosting productivity growth, from the present depressed pace, would also help.

Enhancing resilience in the aftermath of shocks

The long period that the Dutch economy took to recover from stagnation is a testimony to its recurrent vulnerabilities in the aftermath of shocks. In addition to the special factors discussed above that exacerbated the recent stagnation, the economy displays a lack of responsiveness. The reactivity of inflation to slack occurs slowly and with a significant lag, during both the expansion and downturn phases of the business cycle (Figure 1.2). While excess demand pressures began to emerge from 1996, core inflation accelerated only two years later. Similarly, core inflation[1] stopped accelerating only two years after the output gap peaked. The same pattern is evident in the downturn, with core inflation stuck at around 1½ per cent until recently, despite increasingly negative output gaps since mid-2002.

Figure 1.2. **Inflation, core inflation and output gap developments**

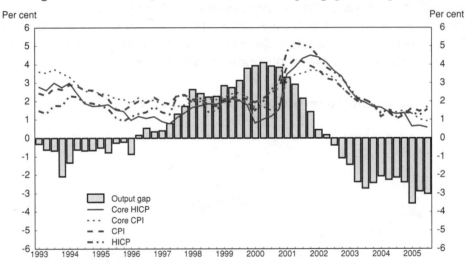

Source: OECD Outlook No. 78 database and OECD, *Main Economic Indicators.*

Like inflation, unit labour costs have been slow to react to cyclical developments. Their weak reaction has caused price competitiveness to evolve pro-cyclically, exacerbating the boom-bust pattern of the recent cycle (Figure 1.3). Indeed, whereas foreign trade contributed strongly positively over the upturn in the 1990s with an accumulated contribution of 13 percentage points of GDP between 1994 and 2000, it contributed only 1 percentage point to GDP growth between 2001 and 2004 (Figure 1.4). While this is partly related to the euro appreciation since 2001, which hit the Netherlands particularly strongly given its larger exposure to non euro-area countries, the main driver behind the loss in price competitiveness (and the persistence of inflation) has been the continued growth of relative unit labour costs well into the downturn.

In fact, low responsiveness of price inflation to excess demand conditions is a long-standing feature of the Dutch economy, as suggested by the empirical work presented in Annex 1.A1. Estimates of an expectations-augmented Phillips curve relationship for inflation show that the elasticity of inflation with respect to the output gap is only 0.18,

Figure 1.3. **Relative unit labour costs in industry**[1]
Year-on-year percentage change

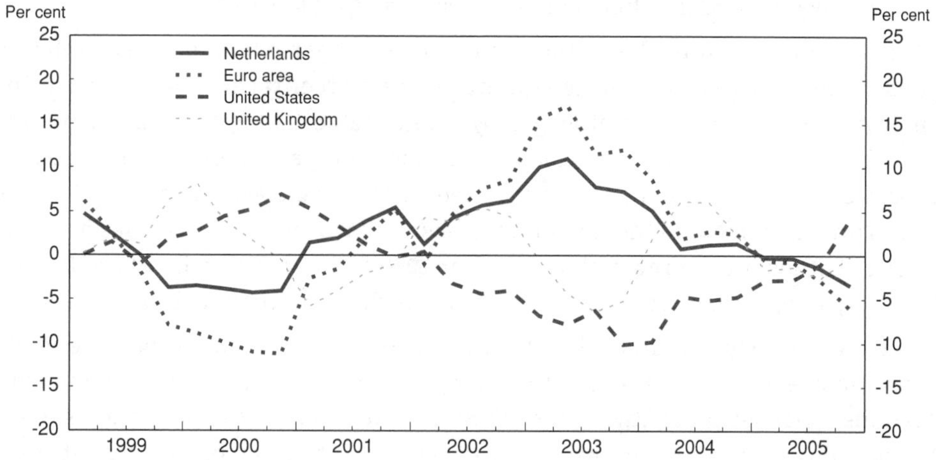

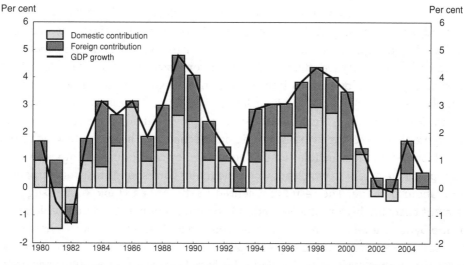

1. Unit labour costs in the manufacturing sector relative to those of competitors, all expressed in dollars. Weights for competitors' costs take into account the structure of competition in both export and import markets of the manufacturing sector for 42 countries. An increase in the index indicates a real effective appreciation and a corresponding deterioration of the competitiveness position. For details on the method of calculation, see Durand, Madaschi and Terribile (1998).

Source: OECD Outlook No. 78 database.

Figure 1.4. **Contributions to GDP growth**[1]

1. The domestic contribution is calculated by deducting the import content from each domestic expenditure component and calculating the contribution to GDP growth. Similarly, the import content is deducted from exports to calculate the foreign contribution.

Source: Kranendonk, H.C and J. P. Verbruggen (2005), "How to determine the attributions of domestic demand and exports to economic growth?", *CPB Memorandum 129.*

i.e., an increase (decrease) in the output gap of 5½ percentage points spread over a number of years is required to reduce (increase) the inflation rate by one percentage point (Table 1.A1.1, column 1). Such a sacrifice ratio is relatively high by international standards. Worse still, it appears that the response of inflation to excess demand pressures is asymmetric, with positive output gaps increasing the inflation rate but negative output gaps having no significant effect on inflation (Table 1.A1.1, columns 2 and 3). Such an asymmetric relationship is also found for France, but not for the other countries (Germany, the United Kingdom and the United States) included in Table 1.A1.1.

Real wage inflation in the Netherlands, on the other hand, is considerably more responsive to changes in unemployment: a one percentage point increase in the unemployment rate reduces real wages by 0.65% (Table 1.A1.2, first panel, column 2), which is broadly in line with the response in most European countries included in the study and only a little less than in the United States. The elasticity of real wages with respect to unemployment in the Netherlands has declined over time, as it has in a number of other countries: in the regression run over 1970-1995, this elasticity was 0.96% (see Table 1.A1.2, second panel, column 2), which was high by international comparison.

A factor that may help to explain high persistence of inflation despite the relatively high responsiveness of real wages to unemployment is that there are large cyclical fluctuations in labour productivity in the Netherlands (Table 1.2) – suggesting significant labour hoarding during a downturn. The average absolute value of the gap between the actual and trend levels of labour productivity over 1970-2004 was 2.1%, more than in any other OECD country. This feature would tend to hold up firms' costs during a downturn and attenuate the rise in costs during an upturn, dampening the impact of the economic cycle on inflation. Gaps in labour productivity have progressively declined over recent business cycles. In the most recent business cycle, the labour productivity gap (1.1%) exceeded the (simple) average gap for OECD countries (0.8%) by a smaller margin than in the previous two cycles.

This cyclical fluctuation in labour productivity reflects the difficulty experienced by firms in adjusting labour inputs to economic conditions. Such difficulty would result in labour hoarding during a downturn, limiting outflows into unemployment. Labour-market rigidities of this kind can be measured using a composite indicator that compares the actual evolution of employment with the evolution suggested by a model where employers and employees are freely able to adjust labour supply and demand in response to any perceived disequilibrium. In such a framework, employment adjustment costs would lead to employment being off the firm's labour demand schedule. The extent to which firms are off their labour demand schedule can be determined by calculating a composite indicator that compares the extent to which actual employment corresponds to labour supply rather than to labour demand. The results presented in the Annex (Table 1.A1.3) suggest that adjustment costs are high in the Netherlands by international standards, which tends to keep employment levels far from firms' desired levels. It should be noted, however, that these results have been obtained by estimation over the period 1970-2004. As shown in Table 1.2, the relative position of The Netherlands in labour market rigidities has improved much since the seventies and eighties. Nevertheless the functioning of the labour market can still be improved. As might be expected, this composite indicator is highly inversely correlated with the strictness of EPL – countries where employment deviates from firms' demand such as the Netherlands have strict EPL. The composite indicator is also highly inversely correlated with the product market regulation (PMR) indicator and with unemployment benefit replacement rates. Regulation that restricts product market competition can contribute to employment deviating from demand by reducing firm turnover and hence turnover in the labour market, which would make it more costly to adjust employment to firms' desired levels. Similarly, high unemployment benefit

Table 1.2. **Average absolute values of hourly labour productivity gaps**[1]

	Business cycles[2]			Average absolute values of hourly labour productivity gaps, 1970-2004
	1970s-1980s	1980s-1990s	1990s-2000s	
A'ustralia	1.0 ('78-'82)	1.8 ('83-'91)	1.0 ('92-'04)	1.1
Belgium	0.8 ('76-'86)	0.7 ('87-'93)	1.1 ('94-'03)	1.0
Canada	1.1 ('70-'82)	0.8 ('83-'93)	0.8 ('94-'04)	0.9
Denmark	2.6 ('76-'81)	1.5 ('82-'93)	0.8 ('94-'03)	1.5
Finland	1.7 ('72-'78)	1.1 ('79-'93)	0.9 ('94-'03)	1.2
France	0.7 ('76-'87)	0.6 ('88-'96)	0.7 ('97-'03)	0.7
Germany	1.4 ('76-'87)	1.1 ('88-'97)	0.4 ('98-'03)	1.0
Greece	na	2.1 ('88-'96)	1.6 ('97-'04)	1.8[3]
Ireland	1.8 ('77-'86)	1.3 ('87-'94)	1.3 ('95-'04)	1.4
Italy	1.1 ('76-'83)	1.0 ('84-'93)	1.3 ('94-'03)	1.2
Japan	1.4 ('77-'84)	1.7 ('85-'94)	0.4 ('95-'02)	1.2
Korea	na	1.2 ('86-'98)	0.8 ('99-'04)	1.5[3]
Netherlands	3.0 ('73-'83)	1.1 ('84-'93)	1.1 ('94-'04)	2.1
New Zealand	3.7 ('70-'80)	1.4 ('81-'92)	0.7 ('93-'04)	1.9
Norway	1.4 ('74-'82)	1.2 ('83-'93)	1.0 ('94-'03)	1.1
Portugal	na	1.5 ('86-'94)	1.4 ('95-'04)	1.5[3]
Spain	1.1 ('70-'85)	1.1 ('86-'96)	0.6 ('97-'04)	1.0
Sweden	1.2 ('72-'83)	0.7 ('84-'93)	0.4 ('94-'03)	0.8
Switzerland	1.0 ('77-'83)	1.9 ('84-'96)	1.0 ('97-'03)	1.4
United Kingdom	0.7 ('76-'82)	1.9 ('83-'93)	0.6 ('94-'03)	1.2
United States	0.8 ('76-'82)	0.4 ('83-'93)	0.5 ('94-'03)	0.6
Average	1.5	1.3	0.8	1.2

1. The labour productivity gap is calculated as the percentage deviation of actual labour productivity from trend labour productivity (HP filtered labour productivity using lambda = 100 and extrapolating the end of the series to 2010 with the Economic Outlook 78 Medium Term Baseline Database). Labour productivity is defined as real GDP per hour worked.
2. Business cycles are measured from the year after a trough, when the negative output gap is greatest, until the next trough. For the last cycle, the final period is 2004 if there is no earlier trough.
3. Labour productivity data for Greece commence in 1983, for Korea 1980, for Portugal 1986.
Source: OECD Productivity database, 2005; OECD Economic Outlook 78 database; Secretariat calculations.

replacement rates – they are the highest in the Netherlands among the countries included in the study – can reduce labour supply following adverse shocks, lowering the gap between the evolution of employment and labour supply.

On the basis of the preceding analysis, it would appear that strict EPL and generous unemployment benefits (reflecting both high replacement rates and long duration of benefits) may be key factors in the lack of resilience of the Dutch economy. Moreover, while barriers to product market competition are around the OECD average, reducing such barriers would also contribute to raising resilience.

Overall, even though there have been one-off factors accentuating the recent cycle, the slow pace at which the economy returns to trend is a longstanding feature of the Dutch economy. Inflation is not very responsive to output gaps in the Netherlands, suggesting that equilibrating forces in the economy are weak. This is not because real wage rates are unresponsive to unemployment, but because firms appear to have difficulty adjusting employment to underlying economic conditions, which forces them to hoard labour in downturns. In addition, the weak reactivity of unemployment to the business cycle reduces the response of real wages to economic conditions. All this limits the decline in unit labour costs, and hence prices, in a downturn and contains the rise in an upturn, weakening pressures for a return to trend output. Thus, strengthening the equilibrating forces in the Dutch economy would entail increasing the responsiveness of employment to economic conditions by easing strict EPL on regular contracts, making real wages even more responsive to unemployment by phasing down unemployment benefit replacement rates as unemployment spells lengthen and removing barriers to product market competition.

Bringing public finances back on a sustainable path

The long period of stagnation has taken its toll on public finances, which went from a significant surplus at the peak of the cycle to a deficit slightly exceeding 3% of GDP in 2003. While cyclical factors played a role, the easing of fiscal policy in the midst of the fast growth period weakened the structural balance of the budget. Cyclical factors accounted for approximately two-thirds of this deterioration while discretionary policy easing accounted for the remainder. To restore public finances, the government has implemented consolidation measures amounting to 1½ per cent of GDP spread evenly over 2003-2005. These measures have successfully cut the budget deficit to an estimated 1.6% of GDP in 2005. With no further reduction in the public deficit planned in 2006 and growth projected to be around the trend rate, the structural budget deficit will deteriorate by about 0.4% of GDP. This will make it more difficult to put public finances on a sustainable path – defined as one where the future costs of government programmes, which are expected to rise substantially owing to population ageing, can be financed at constant tax rates. The Netherlands Bureau for Economic Policy Analysis (CPB) estimated five years ago that a structural budget surplus of 1% of GDP would be required for public finances to be on a long-term sustainable path (CPB, 2000). Developments since then, notably the decline in long-term capital market returns, may result in a higher structural surplus now being required for sustainability.

Hence, budget consolidation is still required to put public finances on a sustainable path. While recent labour market reforms will help to reduce the fiscal challenge of population ageing by shifting some people off social benefits and into employment, these effects are partly offset by the decline in capital-market returns. This is because, faced with lower financial gains, pension funds have to increase tax-deductible contribution rates in order to meet their solvency ratio and/or reduce taxable pension benefits, both of which reduce the net present value of tax revenues. The five-yearly long-term projections of the

CPB, scheduled for release before the end of 2005, will indicate an amount of consolidation required to put public finances on a sustainable path. The policy challenge for the next government (2007-11) is to implement a medium-term policy programme that increases the structural budget balance to the level indicated by the CPB as being compatible with sustainability. This challenge is further discussed in Chapter 2.

Raising labour utilisation to enhance potential growth

Putting public finances on a sustainable path would be all the more easier if trend growth increased from its present slow pace. Trend[2] growth in GDP per capita was 1.8% per year in 1995-2004, similar to the rate in 1980-90 but somewhat lower than in 1990-95 (Figure 1.5). The composition of growth, however, has changed markedly. Trend labour productivity growth has fallen sharply, from 1.9% in 1980-90 to only 1.0% in 1995-2004, while the contribution of growth in labour utilisation, defined as total hours worked per member of the working-age population, has increased. Trend growth in GDP per capita in the Netherlands in recent years has been somewhat lower than in the United States, where the average annual rate was 2.2% in 1995-2004, similar to the rate in 1980-90. In contrast to the Netherlands, there has been a large increase in labour productivity growth in the United States, largely offset by a decline in labour utilisation. With trend growth slower in the Netherlands than in the United States, the gap in trend GDP *per capita* levels, which currently stands at about 25%, is set to widen (Figure 1.6). Indeed, the gap is likely to widen even more

Figure 1.5. Decomposition of average annual growth in trend GDP per capita[1]

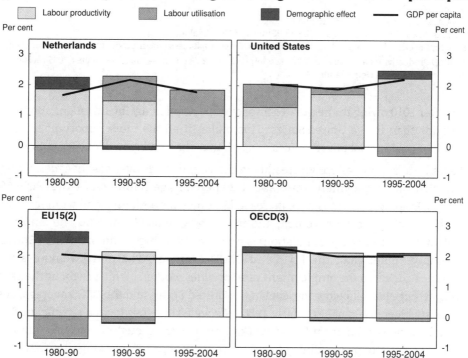

1. Trend calculated by using Hodrick-Prescott filter (lambda = 100). To calculate the trend, the original series was extended beyond 2004 using the OECD Medium Term scenario 2005-2010.
2. Except Austria, Greece, Luxembourg and Portugal.
3. EU15 plus Australia, Canada, Iceland, Japan, Korea, New Zealand and the United States.
Source: OECD Productivity database and OECD Economic Outlook 78 database (includes August 2005 revisions to the National Accounts for the Netherlands).

Figure 1.6. **Decomposition of gap in trend GDP per capita**[1]

Vis-à-vis the United States

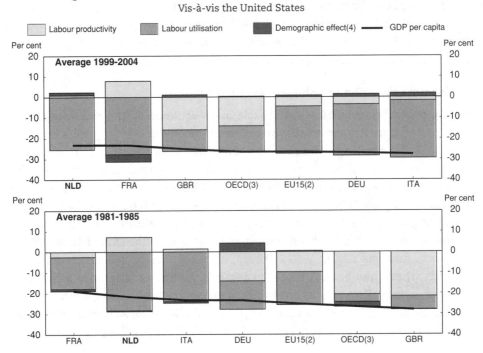

1. US$ constant prices, constant PPPs, OECD base year (2000). Trend calculated by using Hodrick-Prescott filter (lambda = 100). To calculate the trend, the original series was extended beyond 2004 using the OECD medium term scenario 2005-2010.
2. Except Austria, Greece, Luxembourg and Portugal.
3. EU15 plus Australia, Canada, Iceland, Japan, Korea and New Zealand.
4. Demographic effect is calculated as the residual of GDP *per capita* less labour productivity and labour utilisation.
Source: OECD Productivity database and OECD Economic Outlook 78 database (includes August 2005 revisions to the National Accounts for the Netherlands).

quickly after 2010 owing to the greater impact of population ageing on labour supply in the Netherlands than in the United States. This makes it all the more important to raise the utilisation of potential labour resources and enhance the trend growth of labour productivity.

Labour utilisation has grown steadily in the Netherlands over past decades owing to a large rise in the employment rate (about 20 percentage points since the early 1980s) (Figure 1.7). Employment rates have increased strongly for both men and women, although the increase was greater for women, and in all age groups (Figure 1.8). The employment rate (74% of the working-age population) is now almost as high as in the United States and considerably higher than the EU15 and OECD averages. The main weakness in this performance concerns the employment rate for older workers, which is about the same as the EU15 average but far below the level in the United States and the OECD average, despite an impressive increase since the early 1980s. As well, there has been a significant drag on labour utilisation coming from falling working time. Even though the average duration of working time has stopped declining in recent years (Figure 1.9), working time is the lowest in the OECD (Figure 1.10). This factor accounts for the large shortfall in labour utilisation – and hence in GDP per capita – relative to the United States.

Low annual working time mainly reflects the high proportion of Dutch workers (35%) who work part-time (defined as usual working hours of less than 30 per week) (Figure 1.11). This is the highest proportion in the OECD and much higher than in the EU15 (19%) and the

Figure 1.7. **Decomposition of growth in trend labour utilisation**[1]

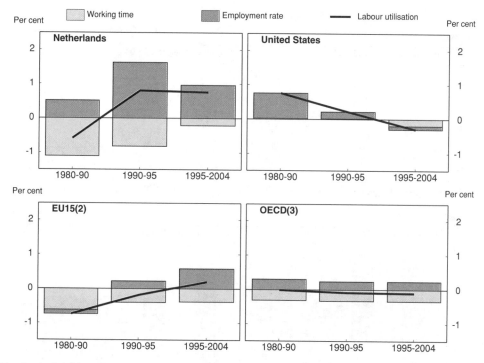

1. Trend calculated by using Hodrick-Prescott filter (lambda = 100). To calculate the trend, the original series was extended beyond 2004 using the OECD medium term scenario 2005-2010.
2. Except Austria, Greece, Luxembourg and Portugal.
3. EU15 plus Australia, Canada, Iceland, Japan, Korea and New Zealand.
Source: OECD Productivity database and OECD Economic Outlook 78 database (includes August 2005 revisions to the National Accounts for the Netherlands).

US (14%). This is largely due to the large proportion of women who work part-time (60% of the total) in the Netherlands, compared with the EU15 (33%) and the US (20%). In addition, relatively many men work part-time and relatively few work 40 hours or more per week by international comparison. The standard working week was cut from 40 hours to 36 hours in the 1980s through agreements made by the social partners. As discussed in Chapter 3, the policy challenge is to increase labour utilisation by increasing incentives to work longer hours, notably by reducing childcare costs and marginal effective tax rates, and to increase the older workers' employment rate by tightening access to publicly subsidised routes to early retirement (disability benefit, unemployment benefit and pre-pension or similar arrangements).

Enhancing productivity growth, especially in ICT-using services

While raising the utilisation of potential labour resources will help maintain living standards, the upcoming ageing of the population makes raising productivity growth all the more important. The Netherlands still has one of the highest level of productivity in OECD, but its growth has decelerated significantly since the mid-1990s (Figure 1.12). Trend hourly labour productivity growth in the Netherlands has fallen from 1.5% in 1985-90 to only 1.0% in 1995-2002. Expressed in terms of trend growth of output per person employed, productivity growth in the Netherlands was the lowest of all OECD countries (apart from Spain) during 1996-2002. The decline appears to be widespread within the economy. The

Figure 1.8. **Employment rates**[1]

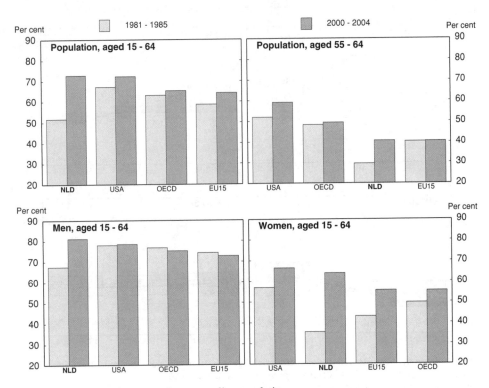

1. Total employment as a percentage of corresponding population.
Source: OECD, Employment Outlook database.

Figure 1.9. **Trend growth in hours worked per person employed**[1]

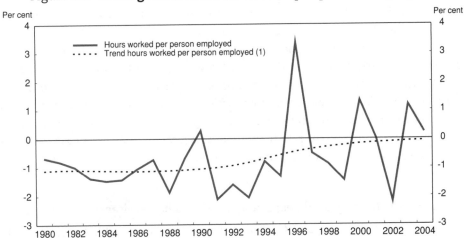

1. Trend calculated by using Hodrick-Prescott filter (lambda = 100). To calculate the trend, the original series was extended beyond 2004 using the OECD medium term scenario 2005-2010.
Source: OECD Productivity database and OECD Economic Outlook 78 database.

sectors that account for the decline in trend labour productivity growth per person[3] in the Netherlands between 1986-90 and 1995-2002 are social services, manufacturing, construction, and agriculture (Table 1.3).[4] The only sector to make a higher contribution was transport

Figure 1.10. **Annual hours worked per person employed**
2004

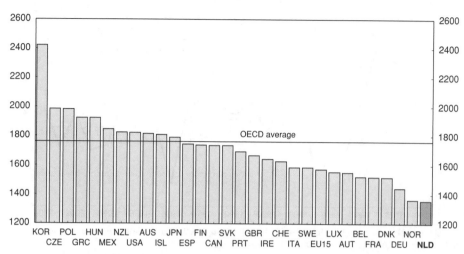

Source: OECD Productivity database.

Figure 1.11. **Distribution of employment by usual working time**
Usual weekly hour bands, 2004

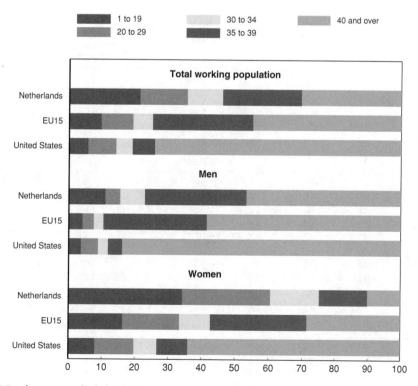

Source: OECD Employment Outlook database.

and communications, where trend labour productivity growth increased markedly;[5] interestingly, both the transport and the communications sectors were liberalised in the 1990s.

Figure 1.12. **Hourly labour productivity growth**[1]

In per cent

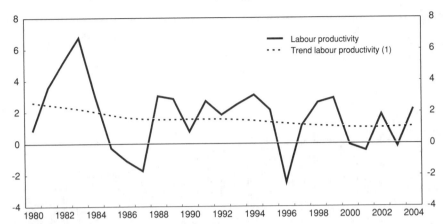

1. Trend calculated by using the Hodrick-Prescott filter (lambda = 100). To calculate the trend, the original series was extended beyond 2004 using the OECD medium term scenario 2005-2010.

Source: OECD Productivity database for hours worked and OECD Economic Outlook 78 database.

Table 1.3. **Contributions to trend labour productivity growth per person employed by sector**

	0199	0105	1014	1537	4041	4500	5055	6064	6574	7599
	Total	Agriculture, forestry, fishing	Mining and quarrying	Manufacturing	Electricity, gas and water	Construction	Wholesale and retail trade, repairs; hotels and restaurants	Transport and storage and communica-tion	Finance, insurance, real estate and business services	Community social and personal services
1986-1990[1]										
Netherlands	1.0	0.2	0.0	0.5	0.0	0.1	0.0	0.2	0.2	−0.1
United States	1.2	0.1	0.1	0.6	0.1	0.0	0.1	0.2	0.4	−0.2
EU15	1.4	0.2	0.0	0.5	0.1	0.1	0.1	0.2	0.2	−0.1
OECD	1.6	0.2	0.0	0.6	0.1	0.1	0.1	0.2	0.4	−0.2
1991-1995[2]										
Netherlands	0.7	0.1	0.0	0.4	0.0	−0.1	−0.1	0.2	0.2	−0.1
United States	1.4	0.0	0.0	0.6	0.0	0.0	0.3	0.2	0.5	−0.3
EU15	1.6	0.2	0.0	0.6	0.1	0.0	0.1	0.3	0.3	0.0
OECD	1.6	0.1	0.0	0.6	0.1	0.0	0.2	0.2	0.5	−0.2
1996-2002[3]										
Netherlands	0.6	0.1	0.0	0.3	0.0	−0.1	0.0	0.3	0.2	−0.2
United States	1.6	0.0	0.0	0.6	0.0	0.0	0.5	0.2	0.8	−0.2
EU15	1.3	0.1	0.0	0.4	0.1	0.0	0.0	0.3	0.3	0.0
OECD	1.5	0.1	0.0	0.6	0.0	0.0	0.2	0.2	0.5	−0.1
Difference 1996-2000 and 1986-1990										
Netherlands	−0.4	−0.1	0.0	−0.2	0.0	−0.1	0.0	0.1	0.0	−0.2
United States	0.3	0.0	0.0	0.0	−0.1	0.0	0.4	0.0	0.4	0.0
EU15	−0.1	−0.1	0.0	−0.1	0.0	−0.1	−0.1	0.1	0.1	0.1
OECD	−0.1	−0.1	0.0	0.0	0.0	−0.1	0.1	0.0	0.2	0.0

1. EU15 excludes IRL and GRC; OECD excludes CZE, ISL, IRL, MEX, POL, SVK, CHE, TUR, GRC, HUN, NZL.
2. 1992-1995 for DEU. EU15 excluded IRL and GRC; OECD excluded CZE, ISL, IRL, MEX, POL, SVK, CHE, TUR, GRC, HUN.
3. 1996-2001 for AUS, GBR, JPN, KOR, NZL, USA. EU15 excludes Ireland; OECD excludes CZE, ISL, IRL, MEX, POL, SVK, CHE, TUR.

Source: OECD STAN database.

In the United States, the increase in trend labour productivity growth (per person) finds its origin in the large contributions from the distribution/restaurants and hotels (ISIC 50-55) and the finance/real estate and business services (ISIC 65-74) sectors, where trend labour productivity growth soared.[6] These sectors, which have in common that they use ICT intensively, account for the bulk of the United States' superior productivity performance in recent years (Figure 1.13). Among them, retail and wholesale distribution made the largest contribution to trend growth of labour productivity, followed by financial intermediation. In the Netherlands, by contrast, the contributions of ICT-using service sectors to trend labour productivity growth barely changed during the 1990s, remaining at levels in 1995-2002 far below those in the United States. As the ICT that made possible such large increases in productivity growth in the United States in the distribution and finance sectors is universally available, it would appear that other ingredients in the recipe for large increases in productivity growth in these sectors are lacking in the Netherlands. Removing barriers to the profitable use of these universally available technologies in distribution and finance is likely to be an important element of any policy measures that succeed in substantially lifting labour productivity growth, notably reforms to heighten product market competition (Chapter 4). Another important element of such policy measures is to improve the innovation performance of the Dutch economy, which is rather weak in relation to its knowledge creation performance. Key policy challenges to enhance innovation activity are to spur business R&D intensity,[7] raise the share of population with tertiary education and intensify the commercial application of new knowledge (Chapter 5).

Figure 1.13. **Decomposition of trend labour productivity growth per person**[1]

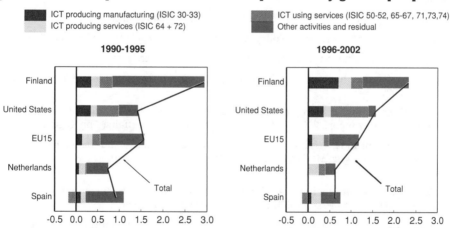

1. Countries are ranked by descending order according to the performance in 1996-2002. Finland was the second best OECD performer (Sweden was the best performer in 1996-2002 but does not provide data for 1990-95). Spain is the worst OECD performer.

Source: OECD STAN database.

Notes

1. Corrected for the increase in VAT in 2001, which added around one percentage point to the price level.

2. Trend has been calculated by applying a Hodrick-Prescott filter with an adjustment parameter of 100 to the underlying series, which were extended beyond 2004 using *OECD Economic Outlook No. 78* medium-term baseline projections.

3. It is necessary to switch the analysis to Labour Productivity (LP) per person employed because hours worked data by sector are not available for the Netherlands before 1995.

4. Contributions are the weighted average of trend growth rates in LP per person employed for each sector. Weights are the annual share of employment in total employment. Trend LP growth per person was calculated by applying a Hodrick-Prescott filter with an adjustment parameter of 100 to the series underlying LP per person employed in the sector (i.e., value added and total employment) extended five years beyond the last period with available data (usually 2002) by the average growth rate over 1990-2002 (or the latest available year).

5. The share of transport and communications in total employment actually declined somewhat, reducing the sector's contribution to overall LP growth.

6. The share of distribution/restaurants in total employment declined slightly, detracting from the sector's contribution to overall LP growth, whereas the share of the finance/real estate services sector in total employment rose, reinforcing the sector's contribution to overall LP growth.

7. According to the OECD *Growth Study,* business R&D spending has a significant impact on long-term growth. More recently, Donselaar, Erken and Klomp (2003) – using the results of a panel study of 22 countries over 1971-1990 by Coe and Helpman (1995) – calculate that an increase of the Dutch business R&D intensity by 10% (representing 0.11% of GDP) would increase the MFP level by 0.8% in the long-run. This would in turn translate into a rise in labour productivity by 1.2%, allowing for the increase of the capital stock needed to maintain the capital output ratio stable. Given its international openness, the Netherlands is also shown to substantially benefit from OECD-wide increases in business R&D through international spill-over effects: a 10% increase in R&D intensity in OECD countries would lead to an increase in the Dutch MFP level by 1.6% and in labour productivity by 2.4%. These results, which are broadly in line with those found in other studies (*e.g.*, as Guellec and van Pottelsberghe, 2001), suggest that the external benefits of innovation activity are high, warranting the considerable attention that OECD governments give to encouraging it.

Bibliography

Coe, D. T., and E. Helpman (1995), "International R&D spillovers", *European Economic Review 39*, pp. 859-887.

CPB Netherlands Bureau for Economic Policy Analysis (2000), *Ageing in the Netherlands*, The Hague.

DNB (2004), "Financial behaviour of Dutch households", *DNB Quarterly Bulletin*, September 2004.

DNB (2005), "Confidence, happiness and financial situation of households", *DNB Quarterly Bulletin*, September 2005.

Donselaar, P., H. Erken and L. Klomp (2003), *Innovation and productivity: a study at the macro, meso and micro level*, summary report, 2003-I-1-03a, Ministry of Economic Affairs, The Hague.

Durand, M., C. Madaschi and F. Terribile (1998), "Trends in OECD Countries' International Competitiveness: The Influence of Emerging Market Economies", *OECD Economics Department Working Papers*, No. 195, Paris.

Guellec, D., and B. van Pottelsberghe de la Potterie (2001), "R&D and Productivity Growth; Panel Data Analysis of 16 OECD Countries,"*OECD STI Working Papers 2001/3*, Paris.

Kranendonk, H.C. and J. P. Verbruggen (2005), "How to determine the attributions of domestic demand and exports to economic growth?", *CPB Memorandum 129*, The Hague.

ANNEX 1.A1

Explaining the Dutch lack of resilience following adverse shocks

Introduction

This Annex presents the results of an econometric investigation of the Dutch lack of resilience. As discussed in Chapter 1, the slow pace at which activity returns to trend following adverse shocks appears to stem, mainly, from the sluggish responsiveness of inflation to changes in the business cycle. Indeed, despite substantial slack having built up in 2003 (when the output gap was about –2¼ per cent of GDP), consumer price inflation was still at 2.3%. The persistence of inflation can affect growth through two channels: it can contribute to keeping monetary policy tighter than would be necessary to support domestic demand; and it can cause a real exchange rate appreciation and depress foreign trade. The Netherlands being a relatively small economy, it is unlikely that it can significantly influence by itself the monetary policy decisions of the ECB. Being a very open economy, however, it is likely that a real exchange rate appreciation causes activity to slacken significantly; indeed, foreign trade only made a small contribution to activity growth in the past five years, as relative prices evolved unfavourably and competitiveness deteriorated.

To explore the persistence of inflation, three separate econometric exercises are presented in this Annex. First, Philips curves estimates are used to assess the sensitivity of inflation to the output gap; they show that this sensitivity is low by international standards in the Netherlands (i.e., the sacrifice ratio is high) and that inflation seems to react asymmetrically, responding more slowly when activity falls below potential than when it moves above it. Second, wage equations are estimated to test a possible lack of responsiveness of real wages to the business cycle; this shows that, in fact, real wages do respond quite strongly. Finally, a model describing labour market rigidities suggests that firms are unable to adjust their level of employment quickly during the downswings due to the lack of flexibility of certain labour market institutions, notably due to the strictness of employment protection.[1]

Assessing the sacrifice ratio

Philips curves are commonly used to assess the reactivity of inflation to aggregate demand imbalances.[2] They can be used to calculate the sacrifice ratio and give an assessment of the cumulative loss of output necessary to reduce inflation by 1 percentage point. The shape of the Philips curve and the sacrifice ratio are likely to be affected by institutional factors, notably rigidities on labour and product markets. In order to estimate the sacrifice ratio, the following specification of the (backward-looking expectation) Philips curve has been estimated and its coefficients compared to those for Germany, France, the United Kingdom and the United States:

$$\pi_t = \alpha + \beta(L)\pi_t + \gamma Gap_{t-1} + \delta(L)Exo_t + \varepsilon_t$$

Where π_t is the quarterly inflation rate, L is the lag operator,[3] Gap_{t-1} the lagged output gap and Exo_t stands for different exogenous factors, notably changes in import prices and in labour productivity (Table 1.A1.1). Moreover, in a second specification (equation 2 for each country), periods of above and below trend growth have been separated by differentiating between positive and negative output gaps and estimating two separate coefficients γ_1 and γ_2. Import price inflation is expected to increase inflation rates (hence a positive coefficient is expected). As to productivity growth, it is expected to lower inflation but the size of its impact depends on the type and degree of competition in product markets: with weak competitive forces, firms may capture parts of the gains from productivity growth for themselves, while with strong competition firms are likely to hand over their cost savings to customers, thereby lowering inflation more forcefully.

The econometric results suggest that inflation reacts weakly to changes in demand imbalances in the Netherlands, compared with the United States or other EU countries (Germany, France, and the United Kingdom). In both the basic and the extended specification (equations 1 and 3), the Dutch sacrifice ratio (5.6 and 6.6, respectively) is considerably higher than those of the other countries (which range from 2.1 in the basic specification for the United Kingdom to 3.7 for the United States, again in the basic specification).What is more, asymmetries can be detected in the case of the Netherlands, with the coefficient for the negative output gap being statistically not different from zero, an indication of a lack of inflation responsiveness in the presence of weak aggregate demand (this is also true for France). This contrasts with the results for the United States where both negative and positive output gaps exercise pressure on inflation or with the situation in Germany and the United Kingdom, where prices are more reactive to weak demand than to strong demand conditions. As regards the additional variables (specification 2), import prices have a statistically significant impact only in the Netherlands and the United Kingdom (with the expected sign), whereas productivity growth lowers inflation in all countries (albeit only at a 10% significance level for France and the United States).

Are real wages flexible?

The slow responsiveness of inflation to slack may result from real wage rigidity. The second econometric estimate presented here therefore evaluates the sensitivity of real wages to labour market conditions. Wage equations are estimated for 17 OECD countries, for the periods 1970 to 1995 and 1970 to 2004, using annual data (Table 1.A1.2). The wage equations are based on the following specification taken from OECD (1997) and Blanchard and Katz (1997):

$$\Delta w_t = a + \beta\pi_t + (1-\beta)\pi_{t-1} + \lambda(w_{t-1} - p_{t-1} - x_{t-1}) - \gamma U_{t-1} + \delta Exo_{t-1} + \varepsilon_t$$
$$\Leftrightarrow \quad \Delta w_t - \pi_{t-1} = a + \beta\Delta\pi_t + \lambda(w_{t-1} - p_{t-1} - x_{t-1}) - \gamma U_{t-1} + \delta Exo_{t-1} + \varepsilon_t$$

Table 1.A1.1. **Phillips curve estimates for the Netherlands, other selected European countries and the USA**

Dependent variable π_t

		Gap(t − 1)	Negative Gap(t − 1)	Positive Gap (t − 1)	Import prices (t − 1)	Productivity (t − 1)	Adj. R^2	Breusch-Godfrey LM test (5 lags)	No. of observations	Time period	Lags included
Germany	(1)	0.277***	–	–	–	–	0.48	F(6, 145) = 0.934	155	1966:Q1-	1, 4, 6
		(4.13)	–	–	–	–	–	P > F = 0.47	–	2004:Q4	–
	(2)	–	−0.390**	0.197*	–	–	0.48	F(6, 144) = 0.948	155	1966:Q1-	1, 4, 6
		–	(2.59)	(1.70)	–	–	–	P > F = 0.46	–	2004:Q4	–
	(3)	0.300***	–	–	−0.020	−0.057**	0.48	F(6, 134) = 1.301	146	1968:Q1-	1, 4, 6
		(4.29)	–	–	(1.12)	(2.14)	–	P > F = 0.26	–	2004:Q4	–
France	(1)	0.355***	–	–	–	–	0.77	F(8, 121) = 1.660	135	1971:Q1-	1, 2, 4, 6, 8
		(3.48)	–	–	–	–	–	P > F = 0.12	–	2004:Q4	–
	(2)	–	−0.135	0.746***	–	–	0.77	F(8, 120) = 1.761	135	1971:Q1-	1, 2, 4, 6, 8
		–	(0.86)	(3.18)	–	–	–	P > F = 0.09	–	2004:Q4	–
	(3)	0.399***	–	–	0.012	−0.103*	0.78	F(8, 119) = 2.002	135	1971:Q1-	1, 2, 4, 6, 8
		(3.78)	–	–	(1.18)	(1.74)	–	P > F = 0.05	–	2004:Q4	–
Netherlands	(1)	0.177***	–	–	–	–	0.40	F(3, 125) = 1.422	132	1971:Q4-	1, 2, 3
		(2.84)	–	–	–	–	–	P > F = 0.24	–	2004:Q4	–
	(2)	–	−0.056	0.290**	–	–	0.41	F(3, 124) = 1.695	132	1971:Q4-	1, 2, 3
		–	(0.46)	2.47)	–	–	–	P > F = 0.17	–	2004:Q4	–
	(3)	0.152**	–	–	0.040***	−0.45**	0.46	F(3, 123) = 0.817	132	1971:Q4-	1, 2, 3
		(2.54)	–	–	(3.18)	(2.28)	–	P > F = 0.49	–	2004:Q4	–
United Kingdom	(1)	0.467**	–	–	–	–	0.66	F(5, 129) = 2.151	139	1970:Q1-	1, 2, 4, 5
		(3.11)	–	–	–	–	–	P > F = 0.06	–	2004:Q4	–
	(2)	–	−0.503**	0.412	–	–	0.66	F(5, 128) = 2.160	139	1970:Q1-	1, 2, 4, 5
		–	(2.18)	(1.37)	–	–	–	P > F = 0.06	–	2004:Q4	–
	(3)	0.414**	–	–	0.101***	−0.237**	0.69	F(5, 128) = 1.772	139	1970:Q1-	1, 2, 4, 5
		(2.88)	–	–	(3.41)	(3.10)	–	P > F = 0.12	–	2004:Q4	–
United States	(1)	0.273***	–	–	–	–	0.51	F(3, 156) = 1.400	162	1964:Q1-	1, 3
		(4.69)	–	–	–	–	–	P > F = 0.324	–	2004:Q4	–
	(2)	–	−0.223**	0.341***	–	–	0.51	F(3, 155) = 1.264	162	1964:Q1-	1, 3
		–	(2.31)	(2.84)	–	–	–	P > F = 0.29	–	2004:Q4	–
	(3)	0.279***	–	–	0.006	−0.083*	0.51	F(3, 154) = 1.074	162	1964:Q1-	1, 3
		(4.72)	–	–	(0.45)	(1.87)	–	P > F = 0.36	–	2004:Q4	–

Note: The table presents the Phillips curve estimates for the Netherlands in comparison with those for Germany, France, the United Kingdom and the USA, using quarterly data. Dependent variable is annualised quarterly CPI inflation for Germany and the USA and annualised quarterly HICP for France, the Netherlands and the United Kingdom, regressed on its own lags, the lagged output gap, lagged import prices inflation (by one quarter), and lagged labour productivity growth. The sum of lagged inflation coefficients has been constrained to one, up to eight lags have been chosen on the basis of their significance level and autocorrelation of residuals. T-statistics are given in parentheses and significance levels indicated by asterisks, with ***: 1% significance level, **: 5% level and *: 10% level. Breusch-Godfrey Lagrange-Multiplier tests for autocorrelation in the residuals have been reported.

In order to test for the asymmetry of the Phillips curve with respect to negative vs. positive output gaps (see Cournède et al. 2005 for a discussion of this approach), the specification (2) includes the two parts of the output gap separately. F-tests for parameter equality between negative and positive output gaps (not shown here) indicate that asymmetry can be assumed for France and the Netherlands but not for Germany, the United Kingdom and the USA, i.e., prices react as strongly to negative as to positive output gaps in the latter countries, while in the former ones, inflation is downward sticky.

Source: Secretariat's estimations.

representing a traditional expectations augmented Phillips curve including an error correction term, λ, based on the deviation of real wages from trend productivity levels, x_t. In this specification nominal wage growth, Δw_t, is a function of the level of the unemployment rate, U_t, (adaptively formed) expected inflation, $\beta\pi_t - (1 - \beta)\pi_{t-1}$ and other exogenous factors, Exo_{t-1}.[4] Other variables included are: i) the difference between the growth in the GDP and private consumption deflators; and ii) an error-correction term, necessary for most European countries, Australia, Canada and Japan to account for co-

Table 1.A1.2. **Aggregate wage equations**

Dependent variable: Growth of real wage ($\Delta(w_t - Pcp_{t-1})$)

1970-2004

	Constant	U	Ln(U)	$\Delta\pi_t$	Pgdp-pcp	Error Correction	Prod. Gap	Adj. R^2	DW
Australia	1.33**	−0.73***	–	–	–	−0.12**	–	0.25	1.69
Austria	0.04***	−0.59***	–	–	1.62***	–	–	0.76	1.22
Belgium	0.08***	−0.78***	–	0.56***	–	–	–	0.80	2.17
Canada	2.69**	−0.43**	–	0.80***	–	−0.25**	–	0.50	1.50
Germany[1]	1.75***	−1.05***	–	–	–	−0.17***	–	0.65	2.60
West Germany[2]	–	–	–	–	–	–	–	–	–
Denmark	0.03***	−0.37***	–	0.69***	0.67***	–	–	0.61	1.82
Finland	0.00	−0.50***	–	–	0.77***	−0.08*	–	0.39	1.60
France	1.17***	−0.60***	–	0.69***	–	−0.11***	–	0.93	1.82
Italy	0.06***	−0.56***	–	–	0.49*	–	–	0.55	1.83
Japan	6.36***	–	−0.08***	–	–	−0.41***	–	0.58	1.33
Luxembourg	2.67***	−1.39***	–	0.92***	–	−0.25***	–	0.58	2.18
Netherlands	**0.04***	**−0.65***	–	–	–	–	–	**0.19**	**1.22**
Norway	2.54***	−0.92***	–	–	–	−0.20***	–	0.46	1.58
Portugal	0.09***	−1.35***	–	–	–	–	–	0.50	1.66
Sweden	3.15***	–	−0.03***	–	0.60**	−0.24***	–	0.37	1.55
United Kingdom	2.20**	−0.25**	–	–	0.67***	−0.22**	–	0.38	1.45
United States	0.06***	−0.76***	–	–	–	–	−0.02**	0.50	1.43

1970-1995

	Constant	U	Ln(U)	$\Delta\pi_t$	Pgdp-pcp	Error Correction	Prod. Gap	Adj. R^2	DW
Australia	1.76**	−0.86***	–	–	–	−0.16*	–	0.29	1.73
Austria	0.02**	−1.71***	–	–	1.31***	−0.34***	–	0.83	1.20
Belgium	1.42*	−0.63***	–	0.60***	–	−0.13*	–	0.87	2.12
Canada	2.68**	0.54**	–	0.69**	–	−0.25**	–	0.56	1.71
Germany[1]	–	–	–	–	–	–	–	–	–
West Germany[2]	3.31***	−0.67***	–	0.83***	–	−0.31***	–	0.90	1.81
Denmark	0.03***	−0.39***	–	0.69***	0.63**	–	–	0.64	1.72
Finland	−0.05	−0.79***	–	0.96***	0.68*	−0.19*	–	0.72	1.40
France	0.02**	−0.74***	–	0.68***	–	−0.12***	–	0.95	2.14
Italy	3.61***	−0.87***	–	–	0.77***	−0.34***	–	0.74	2.34
Japan	4.97***	–	−0.13***	–	–	−0.32***	–	0.68	1.68
Luxembourg	3.06***	−2.31**	–	0.81**	–	−0.28***	–	0.62	2.59
Netherlands	**3.87***	**−0.96***	–	–	–	**−0.38***	–	**0.52**	**1.45**
Norway	1.77**	−0.69*	–	–	–	−0.14**	–	0.15	1.82
Portugal	0.11***	−1.61***	–	–	–	–	–	0.58	1.89
Sweden	2.65**	–	−0.03***	–	0.52**	−0.20**	–	0.43	1.34
United Kingdom	3.04**	−0.27**	–	–	0.72**	−0.30**	–	0.41	1.40
United States	0.06***	−0.82***	–	–	–	–	−0.09**	0.44	1.66

1. Germany 1991-2004.
2. West Germany 1970-1991.

Note: The table presents wage curve estimates for 17 OECD countries both for the period 1970-2004 and 1970-1995 using annual data. The wage equations are based on the specification discussed in OECD (1997), where the dependent variable are nominal wages (w_t) deflated by lagged consumer price inflation (Pcp_{t-1}). Explanatory variables are unemployment (U_t) either in absolute or logarithmic ($\ln(U_t)$) value, the acceleration of consumer price inflation ($\Delta\pi_t$), the difference between GDP deflator inflation and Consumer price inflation ($DPgdp_t - DPcp_t$) and an Error correction term, necessary for most European countries, Australia, Canada and Japan to account for co-integration between real wage inflation and unemployment. For the USA, the change in the difference between actual and trend labour productivity (as measured by a Hodrick Prescott-filter) growth has been found to be significant as well (DProd. Gap). P-values are given in parentheses, asterisks indicate the significance level, where: ***: 1%, **: 5%, *: 10%.

Source: Secretariat estimations.

integration between real wage inflation and unemployment, *iii)* the change in the difference between actual and trend labour productivity (as measured by an Hodrick Prescott-filter) for the United States. The variable measuring the gap between GDP and private consumption deflators reflects the fact that employees are interested in wage rates relative to consumer prices while employers are interested in wage rates deflated by output prices. The expected sign of this variable is positive. Finally, the error-correction term implies that real wages adjust over time towards a level determined by trend productivity and the unemployment rate.[5]

The results presented in Table 1.A1.2 suggest that real wage rate inflation in the Netherlands is responsive to changes in unemployment: a one percentage point increase in the unemployment rate reduces real wage rate inflation by 0.65%, which is broadly in line with the response in most European countries included in the study and only a little less than in the United States. The elasticity of real wage inflation with respect to unemployment in the Netherlands has declined over time, as it has in a number of other countries: in the regression run over 1970-1995, this elasticity was 0.96%, which was high by international comparison. At the same time, the error correction term, defined as the difference between the lagged real wage rate and lagged labour productivity, is no longer significant[6] when the regression is run over the entire observation period (1970-2004). This is a positive development as it implies that factors that decrease the wages that firms can afford to pay conditional on the level of technology, such as energy prices, interest rates and payroll taxes, no longer affect the NAIRU.[7]

Evaluating employment adjustment costs

Even though real wages may be responsive to changes in unemployment, unemployment itself may react to changes in the business cycle only with a lag. This is particularly the case if firms are unable to adjust their workforce freely, due to rigidities embedded in the settings of labour market institutions. The high value of EPL can be taken as an indicator of relatively high costs of employment adjustment, but there are other structural policies that also have an influence. Measuring the reactivity of employment with respect to shocks hence requires the construction of a composite indicator of employment adjustment costs that summarizes the effects of different structural policies.

One possible way to build such an indicator consists of measuring the disequilibrium that may exist between labour demand and labour supply (derived from a calibrated inter-temporal macroeconomic model) as follows:

$$\omega = \arg\min \sum_t \left[n_t - \left(\omega n_t^d + (1-\omega) n_t^s \right) \right]^2$$

where ω is measuring the extent to which employment is supply rather than demand determined and n^d and n^s the revealed optimal choices for labour demand and labour supply by firms and households, which may be based on a standard optimisation framework (for details see Semmler and Gong, 2005, Ch. 8).

The results presented in Table 1.A1.3 suggest that adjustment costs are high in the Netherlands by international standards (ω parameter close to zero), which tends to keep employment levels far from firms' desired levels. The contrast is particularly striking with the United States, the United Kingdom and Ireland, where the ω parameter is much higher – employment deviates less from labour demand in these countries.

Table 1.A1.3. **Composite indicator for labour market rigidities (ω)[1]**

	Omega[2] (ω)	EPL[3]	PMR[4]	UB generosity[5]
Austria	0.22	2.4	1.8	32.9
Belgium	0.24	2.5	2.1	39.0
Canada	0.21	1.1	1.4	15.3
Germany	0.26	2.6	1.9	26.7
Spain	0.20	3.0	2.3	30.3
Finland	0.13	2.2	2.1	33.5
France	0.10	2.8	2.5	36.9
United Kingdom	0.34	1.0	1.1	16.6
Ireland	0.32	1.1	1.5	29.1
Italy	0.13	3.1	2.8	34.5
Japan	0.14	1.9	1.9	12.2
Netherlands	**0.07**	**2.3**	**1.8**	**52.2**
Norway	0.19	2.7	1.8	41.3
Sweden	0.21	2.6	1.8	24.3
United States	0.40	0.7	1.3	13.6
EU[6]	0.20	2.3	1.9	32.4
Average	0.21	2.1	1.9	29.2
Correlation with ω		−0.67***	−0.69***	−0.57**

1. The composite indicator for labour market rigidities has been calculated as the predictor that minimises the difference between the weighted average of labour supply, n^s, and labour demand, n^d, on the one hand, and actually observed employment on the other. Optimal labour demand and supply are derived from an inter-temporal optimising framework following Semmler and Gong (2005). Differences in hours worked have been accounted for by taking total hours worked as the reference value for both labour demand and labour supply. In addition the table reports the OECD-indicators for the strictness of employment protection legislation, the level of wage bargaining coordination, the unionisation rates, the tightness of product market regulation and unemployment benefit (UB) generosity.
2. Omega measures the deviation of actual employment from the level of employment optimally desired by firms on average during 1970-2004. The indicator varies from 0 to 1, with 0 signalling that the level of employment is equal to the supply of labour desired by households and 1 signalling that it is equal to the demand of labour by firms.
3. EPL indicator varies from 0 to 6, with 0 being the least restrictive. The indicator refers to the value of Version 2 in the later 1990s.
4. The product market regulation indicator. It varies from 0 to 6, with 0 being the least restrictive.
5. Unemployment benefit replacement rate average over a five-year period for three family types, value for 1999.
6. Average of above EU countries.

Source: Secretariat estimations, *OECD Employment Outlook* 2003 and 2004, and Conway, P., Janod, V. and Nicoletti, G. (2005), "Product Market Regulation in OECD Countries, 1998 to 2003", *OECD Economics Department Working Paper*, No. 419.

As might be expected, this composite indicator is highly inversely correlated with the strictness of EPL – countries where employment deviates from firms' demand, such as the Netherlands, tend to have strict EPL. The composite indicator is also highly inversely correlated with the product market regulation (PMR) indicator and with unemployment benefit replacement rates. Regulation that restricts product market competition can contribute to employment deviating from demand by reducing firm turnover and hence turnover in the labour market, which would make it more costly to adjust employment to firms' desired levels. Similarly, high unemployment benefit replacement rates – they are the highest in the Netherlands among the countries included in the study – can reduce labour supply following adverse shocks, lowering the gap between the evolution of employment and labour supply.

ANNEX 1.A2

Progress in structural reform

This annex reviews actions taken to follow structural policy recommendations modes in the *2004 OECD Economic Survey of the Netherlands* and, where indicated, still outstanding from earlier *Surveys*. Recommendations made in this Survey are shown in the boxes at the end of each chapter.

Past recommendations	Actions taken and current assessment
A. Labour market	
Disability benefit	
Strengthen the reform of partial disability benefit (DB) by reducing the duration of first-stage benefits, which is the same as for unemployment benefit (UB), and prevent topping up of partial disability benefit.	The maximum duration of first-stage disability benefit will be cut from 5 years to 38 months in October 2006. Action is still required to prevent topping up of partial disability benefit.
Social benefits for the unemployed and means-tested benefits	
Reduce the duration of unemployment benefit.	The government plans to lower the maximum duration of unemployment benefit from 5 years to 38 months in October 2006. The impact of the reform of the UB-scheme on its use as an exit-route to early retirement should be closely monitored. Even after the reform, the maximum duration of the benefit is relatively long compared with other countries, where duration of 1-2 years is more usual
Increase the minimum work record required for access to unemployment benefit.	The special benefit for persons with short work records is to be abolished and access to unemployment benefit will be denied for people having worked less than 26 out of the past 36 weeks.
Job search requirements for unemployment persons aged 57 ½ should be enforced more effectively.	Since January 2004 older unemployed workers are no longer exempt from job search requirements. However, as a part of the UB-reform, the government plans to dispense older persons with care responsibilities from job search obligations. This may be a cost-effective way to address the increase in long-term care needs, but should be monitored to avoid abuse.
Reduce unemployment traps by cutting welfare benefits and increasing earned-income tax credits.	No action has been taken because the authorities judge that cuts in welfare benefits would not be socially acceptable. While unemployment traps can also be eased by phasing out income-related benefits (including tax credits) more slowly, the authorities' judge that the concomitant increase in marginal effective tax rates further up the income scale would reduce the value of labour supplied more than the reduction in the unemployment trap would increase it. In these circumstances no action is warranted.
Improve efficiency and transparency in the reintegration market by: systematic evaluation of private providers' value-added; and giving reintegration firms the possibility of initiating benefit sanctions.	With respect to social assistance ("WWB"), the municipalities have been given full responsibilities for reintegration services, which has led them to implement "work first" strategies with strengthened work obligations and search requirements. Regarding social assistance, DB and UB, improved cooperation between implementing bodies (UWV, CWI's), municipalities and other parties involved is needed to further increase efficiency. However, action is still required to make the tendering process with providers of reintegration services at the local level more transparent.

Past recommendations	Actions taken and current assessment
Speed up the process of phasing-out fiscal incentives for early retirement schemes. Make the tax subsidies for employees taking their "life-course-savings scheme" savings just before retirement conditional on continuing to work part-time.	Tax incentives for early retirement schemes will be terminated in January 2006. The government should monitor the use of the new individual – life-course-savings scheme and prevent it from becoming an alternative route to early retirement.

Working time

Implement the planned reform of childcare support entailing unified subsidies paid to parents instead of to providers and replacing diverse municipal regulation with national regulation.	The Childcare Act that came into effect in January 2005 pays subsidies to parents and introduced national regulation. The budget for childcare subsidies will be increased by € 130 million in 2006 to reduce the rate at which these means-tested subsidies are phased out. In 2006 the child care financing system will be evaluated. Notwithstanding the 2006 evaluation, the government should consider further reducing the taper rate for withdrawing childcare subsidies as household income rises.

Employment protection legislation (EPL)

Ease strict employment protection on regular contracts to make it easier for groups with low participation rates to get jobs and to accelerate labour-market adjustment to economic conditions. Specifically, limit redundancy pay to 12 months, as planned, and reduce the weight of third parties in dismissals via the Centres for Work and Income (CWI).	The government has announced measures to ease EPL that come into effect in October 2006. They reduce protection for older workers (by ending the last-in-first-out principle) and lower administrative costs of dismissals – unemployment benefit applicants no longer have to show that they resisted being laid off. Nevertheless, EPL on regular contracts remains strict by international comparison. No measures have been taken to limit redundancy pay to 12 months as this is a matter for the social partners to decide. The government should go further in easing EPL on regular contracts by reducing the procedural inconveniences for dismissing a worker and widening the circumstances in which a dismissal is justified.

B. Education and innovation policies	
Give universities more freedom in raising fees to foster competition. Extend the system of student loans repayable at income-dependent rates. Make public funding more dependent on performance.	Action is still required.
Closely monitor the effects of the increases in public support for science-industry of private-public co-operation to speed up knowledge transfer.	These effects are being monitored where possible but the absence of a counter-factual case makes this difficult in most cases. The voucher scheme is an exception as vouchers are randomly distributed to applicants. It has enhanced such co-operation. Evaluation features should be built into more schemes.
Introduce TechnoPartner, the generic tax facility for innovative start-ups co-operating with universities.	Done.
Target public support for start-up finance to innovative firms and reduce the administrative burden for start-ups.	Public support for start-up finance has been channelled more towards innovative firms. Although the administrative burden on start-ups has been reduced, further action is required, as planned.
Evaluate the comparative performance of generic *versus* specific R&D support schemes.	The government has decided that greater weight in support for R&D should be given to specific as opposed to generic schemes. There is still a lack of information on the external benefits of different R&D investments suggesting that any such move should be cautious – there is a considerable risk of government failure.

C. Product markets	

Competition law and related regulation

Make the Dutch Competition Authority (NMa) fully independent and give it greater investigative powers and sanctioning powers.	The NMa has been made formally independent and has been given greater investigative and sanctioning powers.
Re-examine laws and regulations governing the liberal professions with a view to eliminating unwarranted anti-competitive practices.	The NMa is examining the regulations and laws governing the liberal professions. In 2005 the NMa is organising a consultation on their stocktaking of regulations and laws affecting competition.
Ease planning restrictions for large-format retail outlets.	The decision-making power on the location of large retail outlets has been decentralised to provincial and municipalities, with one restriction: there should not be a negative impact on the retail trade structure *verzorgingsstructuur*. Action is still needed to ease planning restrictions for such outlets.

Public sector

Stick to the target to reduce the administrative burden on firms by one-quarter by the end of 2007 and implement the planned initiatives.	The government is on track to reduce the administrative burden by one-quarter by the end of 2007.

Network industries

Local government should privatise their retail activities after electricity and gas distribution networks have been split off.	Government has decided to oblige the sector to split off the electricity grids from the distribution and sale businesses.

Past recommendations	Actions taken and current assessment
Leave the roll-out of broadband internet infrastructure to private parties.	The government has stated that investment in broadband Internet should be left to private parties.
Relinquish golden shares in KPN and the postal operator (TPG)	The Dutch government retains golden shares in the incumbent telecoms and postal operators.
Ensure that the ticketing system, which is owned by the Dutch railways (NS) does not act as a barrier to competition	This is not considered to be a problem.
Consumer protection	
Create more Sector Disputes Committees and a small claims tribunal.	In 2006 a Consumer Authority will be set up to deal with consumer complaints. Action is still required to create sector dispute committees and a small claims tribunal.
Housing market	
Ease tough zoning restrictions on residential building sites and simplify building regulations.	The government has presented its policy on zoning in the National Spatial Strategy (Nota Ruimte). It allows for less restrictive practices and decentralises decision-making authority.
Phase out tax subsidies for owner-occupied housing by shifting incremental housing purchases to the third box in the personal income tax system.	This reform is being considered.
D. The healthcare system	
Increase efficiency and responsiveness by moving to a managed competition system by 2006. Develop quality indicators to help consumers to put pressure on insurers to deliver better services. The costs to consumers of switching insurers should be as low as possible.	The managed competition system will come into effect in January 2006. The Ministry of Health has launched a website for consumers to compare costs and quality of insurers. Further action is still required to reduce switching costs.
Monitor the assignment of Diagnostic Treatment Combinations (DTC, which is broader than DRG because it includes related specialist outpatient services) by specialists to reduce the risk of creep (*i.e.*, the deliberate and systematic shift in the reported case mix in order to improve reimbursement).	The authorities plan to create a Healthcare Authority *Nederlandse Zorg autoriteit*: NZa in January 2006. One of its responsibilities will be to prevent creep.
E. Financial markets	
Corporate governance	
Implement proposed legislation that will anchor the *Tabaksblat* code on corporate governance by a requirement to comply or explain.	Done.
Implement legislation that grants certificate holders unlimited and unconditional proxy rights.	Done.
Take further action if shareholders prove ineffective in moderating remuneration packages of board members.	It seems that shareholders have become more effective and growth in remuneration packages of board members has slowed somewhat. However, the government should monitor whether this is a first step or a one-time occurrence.
Implement proposed legislation to extend the tasks of The Netherlands Authority for the Financial Markets *Autoriteit Financiële Markten* to include supervision of accountancy agencies and of financial statements issued by listed companies.	Expected to be implemented at the beginning of 2006.
Pension funds	
The Pension Act planned for 2006 should include guidelines on reporting standards and transparency in communication and establish supervision on reporting.	The Pension Act planned for 2006 includes these features.
F. Sustainable development	
Climate change policy should be rebalanced to equalise marginal abatement costs. Specifically, the regulatory energy tax should be changed to an explicit carbon tax for energy users not included in the EU's trading scheme with the rate set at the expected price of an emission permit. The authorities should also ensure that support offered to renewable energy and combined heat and power does not exceed the carbon tax rate.	No action has been taken.
The authorities should reduce the significant costs of the MINAS scheme aimed at lowering nitrogen and phosphorous pollution from agriculture. Allowable nitrogen and phosphorous balances should be tightened for soil types that are more susceptible to run off.	As a consequence of a recent judgment at the European Court of Justice on the implementation of the Nitrates Directive, the MINAS scheme will be abandoned as from 1 January 2006.

Past recommendations	Actions taken and current assessment
The authorities should ensure that all abstractions of groundwater, including for agriculture, incur the groundwater abstraction charges levied by central and provincial governments and reflect the full cost of the associated externalities, unless the administrative costs outweigh the benefits.	All provincial authorities operate a system of charges with charges levels that correspond to associated regional impact. For efficiency purposes, abstractions below a certain threshold are subject to notification only.
In order to maximise the present value of the surplus extracted from the gas fields, the government should assess the net present value of different resource management approaches to judge whether or not the "small fields" policy should be maintained.	No action has been taken.

Notes

1. The econometric work summarised in this annex follows the recent strand of the literature, which shows that the rigidity of employment is an element to take into account when explaining sluggish responsiveness of inflation and wide and persistent swings in output (Trigari (2004) and Walsh (2005)).

2. Alternatively, inflation persistence can also be measured using univariate estimates such as the sum of the autocorrelation coefficient if inflation is modelled as an autoregressive process (see Levin and Piger (2004) for an overview of different measures and problems related to them).

3. The sum of the lags has been constrained to sum to unity. Up to 8 lags have been estimated and lags with statistically insignificant coefficients have been dropped.

4. For some countries, the unemployment term enters in log form to take account of a non-linear relationship between wage growth and unemployment.

5. For Australia, Austria, West Germany, Finland (only for the period 1970-2004), Italy, Norway, Sweden and the United Kingdom, the coefficient for the second-order price difference was found to be close to 1. The coefficient has therefore been restricted to 1, i.e. nominal wages are deflated by current prices. For Germany, Japan, the Netherlands, Portugal and the USA, the coefficient was insignificant or close to zero and has been dropped. For Japan and Sweden, the natural logarithm of the unemployment rate has been used.

6. This is also true for Austria, Belgium, and Italy.

7. Blanchard and Katz (1997).

Bibliography

Blanchard, O. and L. F. Katz (1997), "What We Know and Do Not Know About the Natural Rate of Unemployment", *Journal of Economic Perspectives*, Vol. 11/1, pp. 51-72.

Conway, P., V. Janod and G. Nicoletti (2005), "Product market regulation in OECD countries: 1998 to 2003", *OECD Economics Department Working Paper*, No. 419.

Cournède, B., A. Janovskaia and P. van den Noord (2005), "Sources of inflation persistence in the euro area", *OECD Economics Department Working Paper*, No. 435.

Levin, A. T. and J. M. Piger (2004), "Is inflation persistence intrinsic in industrial economies", *ECB Working Paper*, No. 334.

OECD (1997), *Employment Outlook*, Paris.

OECD (2003), *Employment Outlook*, Paris.

OECD (2004), *Employment Outlook*, Paris.

Semmler, W. and G. Gong (2005), *Stochastic Dynamic Macroeconomics: Theory and Empirical Evidence*, Oxford University Press, forthcoming.

Trigari, A. (2004), "Equilibrium unemployment, job flows and inflation dynamics", *ECB Working Paper* No. 304.

Walsh, C. E. (2005), "Labor Market Search, Sticky Prices, and Interest Rate Policies", *Review of Economic Dynamics*, forthcoming.

ISBN 92-64-03669-5
OECD Economic Surveys: Netherlands
© OECD 2006

Chapter 2

Putting public finances on a sustainable path

This chapter discusses the fiscal challenges facing Dutch policymakers in the short and medium-term. After large budgetary overruns at the start of the decade, the Netherlands has successfully reined in the government deficit, thanks to a combination of expenditure restraint and revenue windfalls. The chapter discusses these short-term developments as well as the need to resist renewed pressures for spending increases and tax relief. It also discusses how the existing fiscal framework, which has generally functioned well, could be strengthened. Finally it reviews the medium-term budgetary trends, as the effects of population ageing loom large. It argues that the pension system, despite its many enviable features, would benefit from shifts in parameters like retirement age and replacement rate.

The first part of this chapter discusses short-term budgetary developments, which have seen an impressive fiscal consolidation occur in 2004-05, following the sharp deterioration of the budgetary balance in 2002-03. After having exceeded the Maastricht limit of 3% of GDP, the government implemented packages of measures aimed at scaling back the structural deficit that, together with unexpected revenue increases, helped to achieve a considerable consolidation and reduce the fiscal imbalance to 1.6% of GDP in 2005. This consolidation, owes a lot to the medium-term fiscal framework adopted by the authorities, which aims at controlling central government spending and improving the efficiency of the public sector. The second part of the chapter reviews medium and long-term challenges facing the public finances, as the Netherlands prepares for the consequences of population ageing. The country is less exposed to the consequences of ageing than most other OECD countries, thanks to the substantial pre-funding of its pension liabilities. Even so, significant consolidation will be required to put public finances on a medium-term sustainable path. Recent developments have raised the scope of the required consolidation, notably the recent increase in public indebtedness, which weighs on debt-servicing costs, and lower rates of return on capital markets, which squeeze the financial gains earned by pension funds. Lower interest rates, on the other hand, reduce the debt servicing costs for the government. Various policy recommendations are presented at the end of the chapter.

The short-term challenge: returning to safe budgetary margins

Policy measures have scaled back the budget deficits in 2004 and 2005

After several years of strong budget outcomes at the turn of the century, including a significant surplus of 2.2% of GDP in 2000, the sudden deterioration of public finances in 2002-03 caught the Dutch authorities by surprise. This evolution resulted from a combination of weak cyclical conditions (explaining about two-thirds of the deterioration) and discretionary policy actions (about one-third of the change). It can also be concluded, with the benefit of hindsight, that the structural surplus was overestimated in 2000. In 2003, the public finance deficit slightly exceeded the 3% of GDP Maastricht ceiling and in June 2004 the European Council concluded that the Netherlands was in breach of the Treaty. It recommended that measures of a primarily structural nature amounting to the equivalent of at least 0.5% of GDP per year be introduced to correct the situation.

The authorities adopted consolidation measures (in the context of the coalition agreement as well as additional measures) in 2003, 2004 and 2005 to rein in the budget deficit, comply with the requirements of the Stability and Growth Pact and improve long-term prospects in an environment of population ageing. The 2004 budget contained consolidation measures amounting to 0.5% of GDP, notably an agreement with the social partners to virtually freeze wages both in the public and the private sector in 2004 and 2005 and reduce the size of the government workforce by 10 000, mainly through attrition. The budget for 2005 contained consolidation measures also amounting to 0.5% of GDP on both the expenditure and revenue sides of the budget. On the expenditure side, savings of € 150 million were planned by eliminating a reimbursement of employers' unemployment benefits. The government also decided to reduce the coverage of the public health insurance, abolish a disability insurance scheme for the self-employed and shorten the eligibility to unemployment insurance. On the revenue side, contribution rates were increased for health care[1] (AWBZ) and disability insurance (WAO). Two former government agencies were also made liable to pay corporate tax. These, partly additional, measures were intended not only to raise budgetary savings, but were also tailored so as to have positive incentive effects on the labour market, thereby raising medium-term growth prospects. The reduced coverage of disability and unemployment insurance are, in particular, meant to increase incentives to get a job (Chapter 3). The (limited) rise in contribution rates to the health care and disability insurance schemes will, however, increase the cost of labour, with an adverse medium-term impact of labour demand.

Also included in the 2005 budget was a first cut in the corporate income tax rate from 34.5% to 31.5%, with the aim of further reducing it to 30% by 2007. The reduction in the corporate income tax rate was intended to follow the trend towards lower corporate tax rates observed in several European countries and improve the attractiveness of the Netherlands as a location for foreign direct investment. The tax cut was designed to be revenue-neutral with, for instance, increases in the energy tax enacted to compensate for the decline in corporate income tax revenue. The Dutch authorities recently announced a more ambitious plan to reduce the corporate tax rate to 26.9% by 1 January 2007; this proposal has been submitted to Parliament for approval.

The consolidation packages have produced impressive results. Recent estimates suggest that the consolidation objectives set in the 2004 Stability Programme (as submitted to the European Commission) have been out-performed. The overall public deficit fell more than expected, reaching 2.1% of GDP in 2004 (as compared with a target of 3%) and an estimated 1.8% of GDP in 2005 (as compared to a target of 2.6%), mainly as a result of the spending cuts enacted by the government (Figures 2.1 and 2.2). Unexpected windfalls in tax receipts and revenues from natural gas extraction were also used to reduce the deficit avoiding past pitfalls when they were spent to finance permanent measures. Furthermore,

Figure 2.1. **Government total receipts and spending**
Per cent of GDP

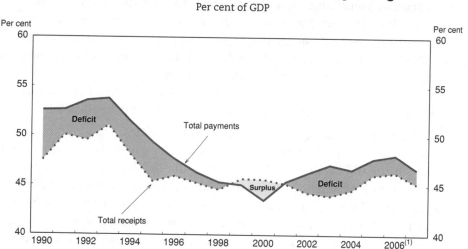

1. The introduction of the new healthcare system increases both expenditure and revenue by 1.25% in 2006.
Source: OECD Outlook 78 database.

Figure 2.2. **Composition of government net lending**[1]

As a percentage of GDP

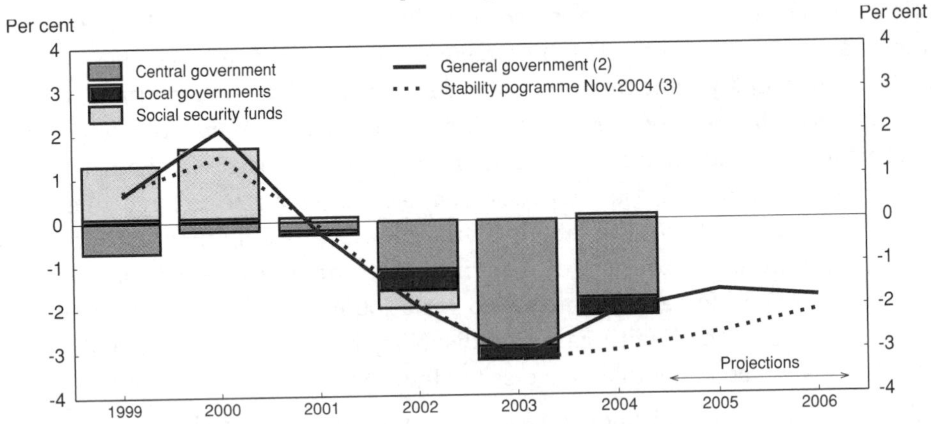

1. New national accounts from 2001.
2. OECD Outlook 78 database.
3. Stability programme, update November 2004, as submitted to the European Commission.

Source: Statistics Netherlands, OECD Outlook 78 database and Stability Programme November 2004.

additional tax increases in 2004 and 2005 also contributed to fiscal consolidation. The EU Council of Finance Ministers has therefore stopped the excessive deficit procedure. As the economic recover gathers pace, the challenge will be to resist demands for additional spending.

The draft 2006 budget, which was presented in mid-September 2005, envisages the government deficit rising to 1.8% of GDP, despite GDP growth being projected above potential, thus halting the consolidation effort undertaken in previous years (Table 2.1). After several years during which real disposable income was under pressure, the government has considered that budgetary prospects have sufficiently improved to introduce measures in support of households' real incomes. The authorities also wanted to reverse the additional tax increases in 2004 and 2005 (compared to the coalition agreement) and help to implement structural reforms (for example health care reform). It has allocated € 2.5 billion for this purpose (0.5% of GDP), of which € 2 billion to cut taxes and social security contributions and € 0.5 billion to increase outlays. As part of this package, more than 6 million households will receive an income-dependent healthcare allowance to compensate them for the higher nominal health insurance premiums resulting from the health insurance reform (Box 2.1). In addition, the budget will make a contribution of € 350 million to avoid the near doubling of a domestic user energy surcharge, which was introduced to finance the development of renewable energy supplies, as part of the government's sustainable development policy (Box 2.2).

The Netherlands benefit from natural gas resources. In 1995, the government decided to establish a separate Fund for Improvement of the Structure of the Economy (*Fond voor Economische Structuurversterking* or "FES") outside the regular budget. The reason for creating a separate fund was to prevent spending of temporary gas related income on current expenditure, because this could undermine the long-run sustainability of public finances and could lead to adverse economic effects. Therefore, over 40% of the gas resources flow into the FES, and should subsequently only be used for investments that strengthen the structure of the economy. As a result, future generations will also benefit from the gas resources. Recent high oil prices have increased the income of the Fund. This

Table 2.1. **Key figures for the general government, 2000-06**

In per cent of GDP

	2000	2001	2002	2003	2004	2005	2006[3]
Government expenditure	**46.2**	**45.2**	**46.0**	**46.7**	**46.2**	**46.3**	**47.9**
Direct expenditure	26.6	26.8	28.2	28.8	28.4	28.6	30.2
Compensation of employees	10.0	9.6	9.8	10.1	10.0	10.0	9.8
Purchase of goods and services (excl. capital formation)	6.3	6.9	7.0	7.2	7.0	7.1	7.4
Fixed capital formation	3.1	3.3	3.5	3.4	3.1	3.0	2.9
Social benefits in kind	7.2	7.1	7.8	8.2	8.2	8.4	10.0
Transfers in cash	15.8	15.2	15.0	15.2	15.2	15.2	15.2
Subsidies (incl. EU)	1.8	1.7	1.8	1.7	1.7	1.6	1.5
Other transfers in cash	14.0	13.5	13.2	13.6	13.5	13.6	13.7
Households	11.2	10.6	10.7	11.1	11.1	11.0	11.0
Corporations	0.5	0.7	0.5	0.5	0.5	0.4	0.4
Rest of the world	2.2	2.1	2.0	1.9	2.0	2.3	2.2
Interest	3.8	3.2	2.8	2.7	2.6	2.5	2.5
General government revenues	**48.4**	**45.0**	**44.0**	**43.5**	**44.2**	**44.4**	**46.1**
Taxes	25.5	24.7	24.5	23.7	23.8	25.0	24.0
Social security contributions	16.0	13.7	13.3	13.8	14.0	13.9	15.6
Non-tax revenue	6.9	6.6	6.2	6.0	6.4	5.5	6.5
Sales	3.1	3.1	3.1	3.3	3.3	3.2	3.2
Revenues from natural gas	0.7	0.9	0.9	0.9	1.0	1.2	1.2
Other revenue	3.1	2.5	2.2	1.9	2.1	1.1	2.1
General government balance (EMU)	**2.2**	**–0.3**	**–2.0**	**–3.1**	**–2.1**	**–1.8**	**–1.7**
State[1, 2]	0.4	–0.1	–1.0	–2.8	–1.8	–1.5	–1.8
Other central government	0.1	–0.1	0.0	0.0	0.0	0.0	0.0
Local government	0.1	–0.1	–0.5	–0.3	–0.4	–0.4	–0.3
Social security funds	1.6	0.1	–0.4	0.0	0.1	0.1	0.4
Gross debt general government (EMU)	55.9	50.7	50.5	51.9	52.5	54.6	54.5
Memorandum items (change in %)							
Real gross government expenditure	1.0	...	1.7	1.5	0.8	¾	6.0
Employment general government	0.8	...	2.1	0.4	–0.7	–¾	1¼
Employment care industry	2.2	...	6.3	5.1	1.9	1½	2¾
Wage rate general government	5.0	...	4.3	4.9	2.9	2.0	½

1. In 2000, this includes the incidental revenues from the sale of telecom frequencies of 0.7% GDP; in 2001, this includes an incidental transfer to the former public corporation DSM of –0.3% of GDP
2. The figures for 2003 are influenced by the introduction of a VAT-compensation fund for local government. Corrected for the incidental effect of this VAT-compensation fund, the financial balance of the local government is 0.3% of GDP lower and the financial balance of the state is 0.3% of GDP higher.
3. The introduction of the new healthcare system increases both revenue and expenditure by 1.25% of GDP in 2006.

Source: CPB Netherlands Bureau for Economic Policy Analysis (2005b).

has been used for a broad additional investment programme, totalling € 2.3 billion over a multi-year period up until 2015 that targets innovation, knowledge and investments in physical infrastructure.

What fiscal framework to foster economic resilience?

The impressive fiscal consolidation achieved in 2004-05 owes a lot to the medium-term framework adopted by the authorities. The "trend-based budgetary policy" framework differs from fiscal rules commonly adopted in other countries, in that it primarily caps public spending in real terms, rather than the nominal budget deficit. The framework, which was introduced in 1994 is based on an agreement between political parties participating in the coalition governments. It consists of limits on real expenditure

> **Box 2.1. Healthcare reforms: impact on macro-economic indicators***
>
> With effect from 1 January 2006, the compulsory public health insurance and private health insurance systems will be merged into a new compulsory – privately administered – basic health insurance system for curative healthcare. The authorities aim to increase efficiency and responsiveness to patient demands by moving to a managed competition system. Health insurance companies will compete through their standard premiums and quality. To this end they can negotiate with healthcare providers about the price and quality of services. Insurance companies will not be able to refuse clients or to charge different premiums depending on their risk characteristics. The existing premiums will be replaced by a flat rate premium for adults (paid by households) and an income-dependent contribution (for wage earners paid by employers), which together should cover half of all healthcare costs. The government will take a number of additional measures aimed at keeping the burden on employers unchanged and reducing it on households, *e.g.*, through an income dependent healthcare allowance, a lower income-dependent contribution for persons without an employer and a reduction in unemployment benefit (UB) premiums. This burden relief should cushion at least some of the considerable income effects which will inevitably accompany this reform.
>
> The reform of the health insurance system has implications for the measurement of a number of macro-economic variables in the national accounts. It will lead to a shift from private consumption to public consumption in volume terms. Statistics Netherlands (CBS) allocates private health insurance premiums to private consumption. Since the privately insured will become part of the public health insurance scheme from next year, the volume of private consumption will decline while the volume of public health consumption – the benefits in kind – will increase. Furthermore, the health insurance funds' unbudgeted administration costs will be allocated to public consumption. In 2006 this will cause a decline in private consumption of 3½ per cent and a rise in public consumption of 6%. The public sector wage bill in real terms will fall because the health insurance funds will in future be included among the private insurance companies. Real GDP will not be affected because the decline in the volume of private healthcare consumption and the increase in public consumption cancel each other out.
>
> * More detailed information on the new healthcare system and the macro-economic consequences can be found in OECD, 2004 (Box 3.2) and CPB, 2005a.

in each major budget sector – the central budget, health care, and social security – set for the duration of the government's term in office. The caps are set in real terms and are adjusted each year for inflation in the context of annual budgets. The limits are based on cautious macroeconomic projections produced by the independent Netherlands Bureau for Economic Policy Analysis (CPB).

The prevailing agreement, which covers the period 2004-07, reflects the ambition of the coalition government to restore fiscal balance, reduce the level of public spending, streamline the tax system and reform the health care sector (CPB, 2003). The coalition agreement aims at reducing net spending by € 8 billion, nearly 2% of GDP, during the 4-year period. Gross spending cuts amount to € 11 billion, of which about half result from wage moderation in the public sector as well as cuts in the size of the public sector workforce. In addition, the rise of social benefits is expected to be indexed to wages in the public sector, rather than wage developments in the private sector. It was also agreed to tighten a number of entitlements, subsidies and social benefits. As well, coalition partners agreed to

Box 2.2. **Promoting sustainable development: renewable energy**

With the deregulation of the energy sector well under way, the government is concentrating on the problems surrounding security of supply and climate change. It regards the realisation of the Kyoto target as a major task. The Netherlands has already been pursuing a climate change policy for nearly 15 years. Renewable energy is taking off, and a first step in the reduction of greenhouse gases has been taken. The government deems that there is a very good chance that the Netherlands will meet its Kyoto target, although this will still require considerable efforts. Measures are aimed at achieving a higher energy efficiency rate, a sustained development of European emission trading and a higher share of renewable energy sources (MEA, 2005).

With regard to the share of renewable energy, a European target has been set at 9% by 2010. This is deemed to be achievable partly thanks to the Act on *Environmental Quality of Electricity Generation* (MEP), which consists of a subsidy scheme for producers of renewable energy financed through a user connection fee. However, the downside of the success so far is that the costs of MEP schemes are rising much more steeply than anticipated. Therefore, the budgetary control over the MEP scheme will be improved with the introduction of subsidy caps and the scheme will offer a multi-year certainty about government support for each project. Biomass and wind energy (both onshore and offshore) are likely to make the largest contributions, over both the short and the long run. To prevent a steep increase in the user connection fee, certain investments in renewable energy, *e.g.*, windmills at sea, will be subsidised from the FES rather than the MEP.

The government is also promoting sustainable development through FES financial support to programmes reducing the Netherlands' dependence on fossil fuels and emissions of greenhouse gases. Some € 250 million has been earmarked for the Borssele nuclear power station, should it be decided to keep it open – a decision that should be made by year-end. In addition, resources will be used for energy saving, clean fossil fuels (*e.g.*, carbon dioxide storage) and renewable energy sources (including innovative biofuels). The intention is to double the climate change benefit – lower carbon dioxide emissions – of keeping Borssele open. As part of the decision-making process, the government is holding discussions with the energy companies on a substantial contribution from their side (MF, 2005).

increase government spending by € 3 billion to finance health care, the knowledge economy, infrastructure building, public order and environmental protection. The agreement foresees a rise in tax revenues by € 3.25 billion (about ¾ per cent of GDP), resulting from the increase in health insurance contributions, tax base broadening and increases in energy taxes.

The adoption of a multi-year fiscal framework that establishes agreed ceilings for public expenditure during the term of office of the government is particularly well-suited to the specific nature of the Dutch political system. Throughout its recent history, the government has been formed by coalition parties, making it impractical to entrust the finance minister with the authority to override the budget demands of sectoral ministers. Fiscal discipline is further weakened by the fragmentation of the budget into twenty-three separate bills, each of which may be amended by Parliament. But, as suggested by recent political economy research, the use of a "contract" between political parties, with strong disincentives to renege on the commitment, is well adapted to coalition governments, as each coalition partners would otherwise attempt to extract private rents for their electorate, without taking account of social costs (Hallerberg *et al.*, 2004).

Furthermore, focusing on explicit expenditure targets or spending caps appears to be more efficient for the purpose of sound public sector management than adhering to nominal budget deficit ceilings. One key advantage of medium-term expenditure targets is that they provide each Ministry with clear prospects about future resources and, knowing them, allows policymakers to concentrate on the quality of public spending rather than its quantity. Also, it enhances the accountability of governments because it implies a transparent benchmark against which performance can be assessed. Together with outcome-based budgeting, expenditure caps can improve considerably the quality of fiscal policy. The framework appears to have helped improve the efficiency of public spending and contributed to keeping the trend of government spending under control, as shown by the retrenchment of the ratio of public expenditure in GDP since the early-1990s (Figure 2.3), an outcome that has not prevailed in all OECD countries. This has resulted in a decline of the debt-to-GDP ratio and a concomitant reduction in average tax rates since then.

Figure 2.3. **Government spending trend**

In percentage of GDP

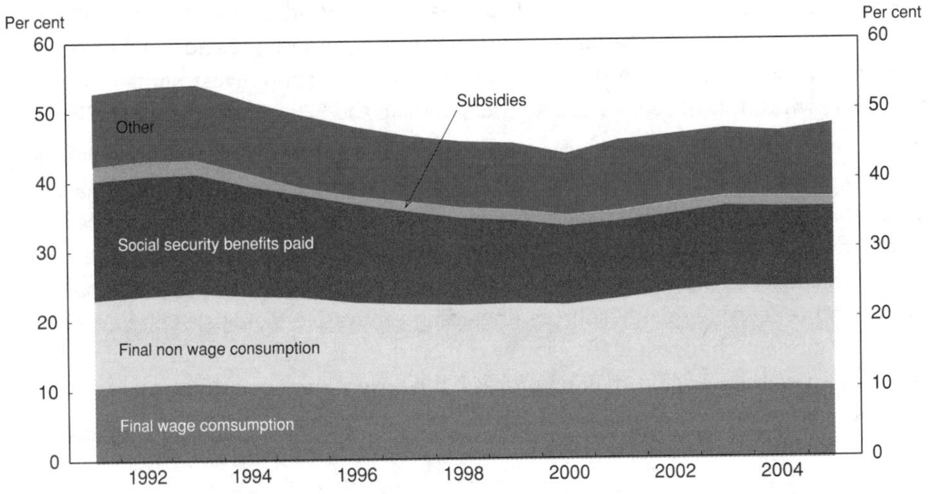

Source: OECD, Economic Outlook No. 78.

Another feature of the present fiscal framework is that, in principle, it allows automatic stabilisers to operate freely on the revenue side of the budget, thus helping to stabilise output in a more effective way than nominal deficit targets. Safe budgetary margins need to be achieved for this purpose, especially in the case of the Netherlands, where the sensitivity of budget balance to changes in GDP is estimated to be high compared to other OECD countries (Figure 2.4), even though this sensitivity has declined in recent years with the decline in marginal income tax rates and the reduced generosity of social benefits (Girouard and André, 2005). The free play of automatic stabilisers is particularly important for an economy that is a member of a monetary union, where monetary policy aims at price stability in the entire currency area and cannot address country-specific fluctuations and asymmetric shocks.

This sound fiscal framework has been, however, severely tested since the late 1990s. Contrary to the prediction that expenditure caps would contribute to output stabilisation, the Netherlands has experienced large cyclical swings and unusually wide output gaps

Figure 2.4. **Cyclical sensitivity of fiscal balances**[1]

In percentage point of GDP

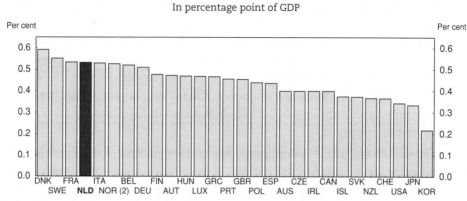

1. The chart shows the change of the budget balance, as a per cent of GDP, for a 1% change in GDP, based on 2003 weights. For the Netherlands, a change of 1% of GDP is accompanied by a change of 0.53 percentage points of the budget balance.
2. Mainland only, for Norway.

Source: Girouard, N. and André, C. (2005), "Measuring cyclically-adjusted budget balances for OECD countries", *OECD Economics Department Working Papers*, No. 434.

over the past decade. In addition, the expenditure limits have not been successful in preventing the budget deficit from exceeding the Maastricht limit. These negative outcomes do not imply that the fiscal framework should be fundamentally changed but, instead, that it should be altered so as to improve its functioning. Several aspects appear to be in need of reform.

The fiscal slippages experienced at the start of the decade reflect, to a large extent, the permanent tax cuts that were decided at the top of the cycle, when the budget unexpectedly benefited from large revenue windfalls, which proved to be temporary, but were nonetheless used to finance permanent tax reliefs and generous real expenditure increases. Unless there are fundamental changes in the tax system, it is unlikely that tax revenue windfalls can last forever and it is therefore good practice to use such windfalls to reduce the deficit, rather than to finance permanent discretionary measures. Similarly, it is good practice to allow tax revenues to decline in recessions – at least when the cyclically-adjusted budget balance is close to a position that is consistent with sustainable medium-term public finances. This is not the case at present, however, and the automatic stabilising properties of tax revenues can be allowed to operate only asymmetrically. The authorities should therefore more strictly abide to a rule that the entirety of unexpected windfall gains be used to reduce the deficit.

The existing medium-term framework has served the purpose of spending control well but, like most policy rules does not attain full coverage of budgetary policy. This creates risks for circumventing budgetary rules by creative operations (Kraan, 2005). One such operation would be the increasing use of tax expenditures to provide benefits and subsidies to targeted groups without increasing spending, which erodes budgetary discipline. Every year the budget memorandum includes a special annex with an overview of tax expenditures which are being considered. According to these figures, there has been a decrease in the number of tax expenditures (from 126 in 2002 to 108 in 2006 and in their overall cost from 3.2% of GDP in 2002 to 2.3% in 2006). Moreover, an evaluation system has been set up, so as to appraise the effectiveness and efficiency of these schemes on a regular basis. Besides these tax expenditures, there are large amounts deducted from taxes for owner occupied housing, although this is partially clawed back through taxes on imputed rentals and property taxes, and of tax revenues forgone from not taxing pension fund earnings as they accumulate and from the fact that pensioners generally pay lower marginal tax rates in retirement than when they made contributions to their pension schemes (taxation is EET). The government provides less information on these amounts than on tax expenditures, although there is information on the amount of interest payments on mortgages in the Budget memorandum (albeit not on a yearly basis) and the amount of pension premiums paid (published by the Central Planning Bureau and the Bureau of Statistics every year).

The revenues of FES (Fund for improvement of the structure of the economy) are not included in the central budget and are not part of the system of spending limits. The FES is mainly funded by Dutch natural gas revenues (and partially by privatisation proceeds), and is invested in projects that aim at strengthening the physical and knowledge infrastructure. The FES was created to use incidental gas revenues to finance investments such as public works. The current high oil prices and higher incomes of FES increase the revenue, which is a risk for the good selection of investment projects. Therefore, this funding system will be reconsidered in spring 2006.

The long-term challenge: returning to a sustainable path

Like other OECD countries, the Netherlands approaches a long process of population ageing, with potentially negative effects on economic growth and the sustainability of public finances (OECD, 2005a). Although there are many uncertainties involved in long-term projections, it is quite well established that the costs of public pension and health care schemes will increase significantly in coming decades, especially in 2030-40. By the middle of the century, the Netherlands may have to pay about 4 percentage points of GDP more than currently for public pensions and about 3 percentage points more for health care spending. This prospect creates obvious uncertainties for the sustainability of public finances, which need to be addressed in a timely manner, not only from the standpoint of financial viability, but also for the sake of intergenerational equity and microeconomic efficiency. The next section of this chapter discusses several typically Dutch institutional features which, according to both official and independent projections, are deemed to make it easier to solve the problem of public finance sustainability in the Netherlands than in other countries. Following recent developments, however, this assessment appears to be excessively optimistic in several respects and, under more realistic and updated assumptions, achieving sustainability is likely to prove more challenging than initially expected. The final section suggests a number of policy recommendations that could be envisaged to bring the public finances back on a viable medium-term path, while allowing for inter-generational fairness and avoiding distortions.

Positive features in the existing medium-term strategy

Compared to other countries, the Netherlands benefits from several features that are frequently seen as making it somewhat easier than in other OECD countries to meet the challenges of population ageing. A first specific feature is that demographic prospects are projected to be less adverse than in many other countries, with the dependency ratio (population of those 65 years old and over to those aged 15-64) projected to rise from about 20% currently to a peak of 43% in 2040, and then decline slightly. The increase in the dependency rate is substantially less pronounced than in many other OECD countries

(Figures 2.5), thanks to the structure of population cohorts. In particular, the Netherlands has had a positive immigration surplus since the early 1960s, which partly explains the slower ageing process (OECD, 2005b). Furthermore, a substantial amount of pre-funding of future pension liabilities has been achieved with the accumulation of savings in compulsory occupational pension funds (provided by employers at the firm or sector level), which hold assets equivalent to about 130% of GDP (Figures 2.6). Also, the government has accumulated a large tax claim on pension wealth, in the form of future payment of income taxes on pensions, which are subject to tax, while contributions are tax deductible ("EET" taxation). These deferred tax assets are officially estimated to amount to 30% of GDP. In addition, the drawdown of pension benefits by future pensioners will raise their levels of income and consumption, thus increasing indirect tax receipts. These two future sources of additional direct and indirect tax revenues are expected to amount to 4 percentage points of GDP, enough to finance about one-half of the increase in ageing-related spending (Van Ewijk, 2005).

Figure 2.5. **Dependency ratios**

Ratio of population aged 65 and over to population aged 20-64

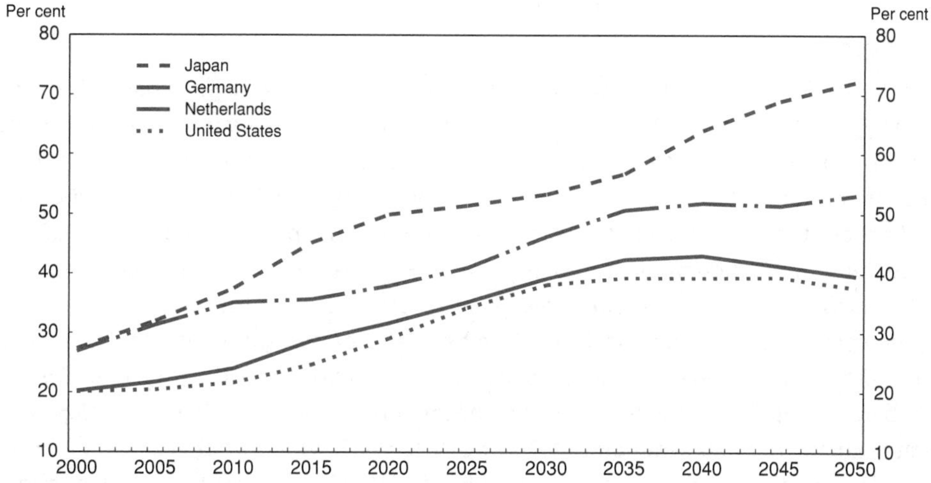

Source: OECD/ELS Population database.

The other half of the financing gap is expected to be financed by the repayment of government debt and the related reduction in government interest payments. Existing projections (CPB, 2000) estimate that achieving a structural budget surplus of at least 1% of GDP during the period 2000-2030 would allow the repayment of almost the entire stock of public debt.[2] This would reduce government interest payments sufficiently to make room for the remaining one-half of the increase in ageing-related spending. This policy of "pre-funding" pension liabilities by accumulating tax assets and achieving budget surpluses is seen by the government as sufficient to restore the sustainability of public finances. This is also seen as being an inter-generationally fair approach, because it does not transfer the burden of pension payments to future generations. It also appears to be efficient from the standpoint of tax smoothing, because it avoids future variations in marginal tax rates and their possible deadweight losses.

Figure 2.6. **Financial assets of insurance and pension funds**
Per cent of GDP

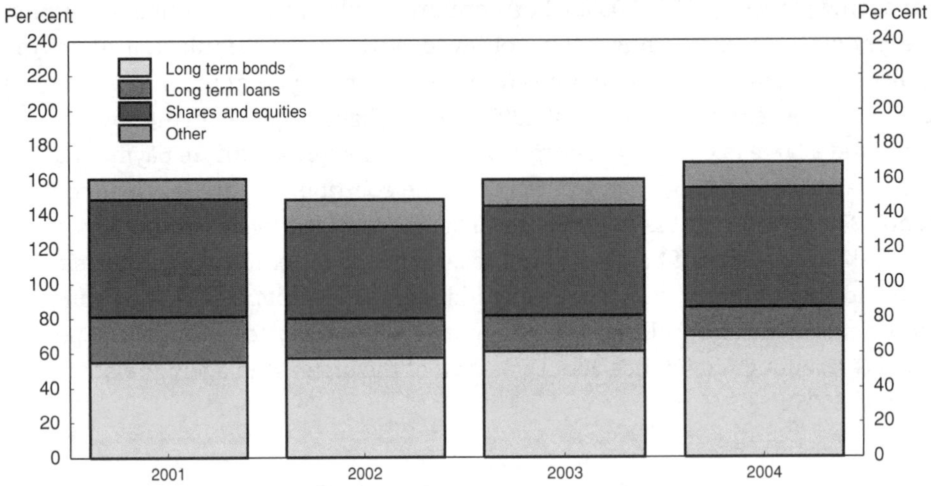

Source: Statistics Netherlands.

Some caveats

These projections need, however, to be reconsidered on a regular basis. Indeed, the projections produced in 2000 by the CPB seem to be in the conservative part of the range – the European commission for instance, estimate an increase in the cost of public pension, health care and long-term care of 9-10 percentage points of GDP by 2050 (EPC, 2001) rather than 7 percentage points. Furthermore, the long-term projections of the CPB were produced at a time when public finances were in surplus and the public debt-to-GDP ratio was declining. Scenarios of sustainable policies called for continuing such trends (CPB, 2000). However, as noted, the fiscal situation has deteriorated since then and the budget is not presently on course to achieving a structural surplus (Figure 2.7A): the November 2004 update of the Stability Programme presented to the European Commission aims at reducing the public deficit to 1.9% of GDP in 2007, which would correspond roughly to a cyclically-adjusted deficit of about 1.2% of GDP. This is significantly less than the surplus of 1% of GDP required to achieve sustainability.[3] Reflecting these accumulated imbalances, government debt increased by about 5 percentage points of GDP during 2001-05, making it very unlikely that the reduction of pubic debt by 26 percentage points of GDP will be achieved by 2010, as was projected by CPB (2000) (Figure 2.7B). It is therefore necessary that upcoming budgets, notably those established under the fiscal framework adopted by the next coalition government (2007-11), contemplate further and long-lasting fiscal consolidation.

Finally, long-term projections are very sensitive to the assumptions of the exogenous parameters. Notably, the projections are based on the assumptions that pension funds earn real rates of return of 4% on bonds and 8½ per cent on equities, well above present rates of return. Lower rates of return would have a negative effect on the budget as the tax-deductible contributions to pension funds would need to be higher and/or taxable pensions would be lower. The upcoming five-yearly re-estimation of long-term projections, scheduled to be released by end-2005 or early 2006, might test the sensitivity of the projection to a different set of assumptions.

Figure 2.7. **Long term public finance projections under sustainable policies**
Per cent of GDP

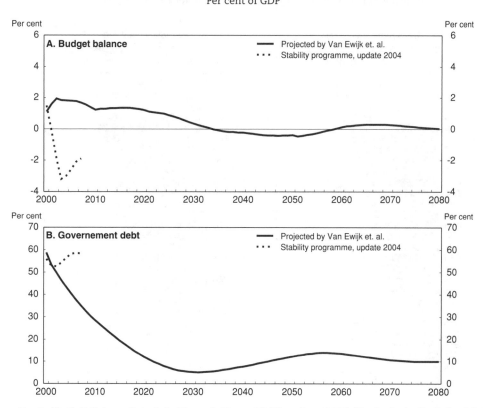

Source: Van Ewijk, C., B. Kuipers, H. ter Rele, M. van de Ven and E. Westerhout (2000), "Ageing in the Netherlands"; CPB Netherlands Bureau for Economic Policy Analysis and European Commission.

Additional policy measures to achieve public finance sustainability

In case a larger structural surplus is needed, this would require tax increases and/or spending cuts that would most probably prove difficult to implement. Large increases in tax rates would entail economic costs, notably negative implications for labour market participation. Large reductions in public spending might be less distortionary than tax increases, but may conflict with the social choices of the Dutch society. Other measures might therefore be needed to achieve long-term financial sustainability. Possible candidates are to lower the present levels of pension replacement rates, which are high by international standards; to raise the labour market participation of older workers; to increase the pension age, and foster economic growth by a higher productivity growth (in combination with a reconsideration of the linkage of public sector income to private sector wages).

The Dutch pension system has ambitious, but also quite costly targets. The two mandatory pension pillars aim at achieving replacement rates close to 70% of pre-retirement gross earnings and net replacement rates to be comprised between 82.5% and 88.2% of net pre-retirement earnings (OECD, 2005c), which are among the highest among OECD countries (Figures 2.8). These high replacement rates require major amounts of resources from the public and private sectors and, although they provide high real incomes to pensioners, may distort individual incentives and imply deadweight losses. The mandatory pension incomes are topped up by revenues from voluntary savings schemes,

Figure 2.8. **Replacement rates at different earnings levels**

Percentage of individual pre-retirement earnings, for an average male earner

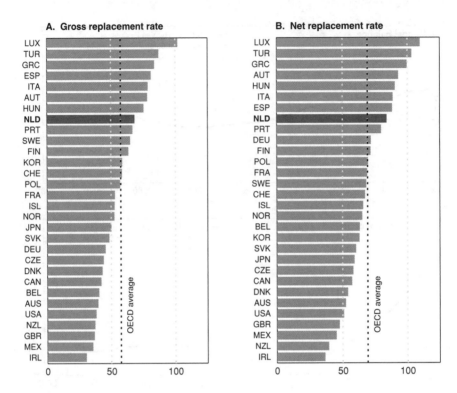

Source: OECD (2005c), *Pensions at a Glance.*

and pension incomes are taxed at much lower levels than earned incomes,[4] so that net pensioner incomes can exceed in certain circumstances the level of pre-retirement earnings. Lowering target replacement rates in second-pillar plans closer to international standards would reduce existing distortions and, with properly designed reforms, could be growth-enhancing.

This would also, according to existing simulations, help the sustainability of public finances. Reducing the levels of pension fund benefits would have two opposite effects on public finances: it would lower contribution rates and therefore reduce the scope for tax deduction, but it would also reduce future tax assets to be collected on pension income. According to simulations of a dynamic general equilibrium model of the Netherlands by Van Ewijk (2005), the former effect dominates the latter one (Table 2.2). For instance, a reduction in the pensions levels from 70% to 60% of final earnings introduced in 2010 would lower public indebtedness by an additional 15 percentage points of GDP (compared to a baseline on unchanged policies). This beneficial effect on public finances mainly results from the fact that earned incomes are taxed at higher marginal rates than pensions, so that reducing tax deductibility of earned incomes more than offsets the tax losses on pension incomes. The government cannot lower replacement rates directly, but changes in key pension fund parameters have moved them in this direction, as discussed below.

Pension schemes have recently changed some of their key parameters. The most notable change has been the shift from final pay schemes (pensions based on last salary)

Table 2.2. **Effects of a reduction in defined benefit pensions from 70% to 60% of final earnings in 2010[1]**

		2015	2025	2050	2100
Pension contributions (% of wage sum)	D	−3.0	−2.6	−1.6	−1.7
Pension payments (% of wage sum)	D	−0.5	−1.6	−3.1	−3.2
Tax revenue (% of GDP)	D	0.1	0.3	0.1	0
Public debt (% of GDP)	D	−4.0	−8.5	−12.8	−14.6
GDP (market prices)	%	0.5	−0.1	−0.3	−0.4
Private employment (labour years)	%	1.1	−0	−0.3	−0.3
Consumption	%	−0.3	−0.4	−0.4	−0.5
Tariff consumption tax	D	−0.1	−0.1	−0.1	−0.1

1. Averages over the preceding five years. D indicates an absolute differential *vis-à-vis* the baseline scenario, % indicates a relative change. Pension replacement rate concerns pensions as a percentage of final pay.

Source: Simulations of the CPB general-equilibrium model GAMMA by Van Ewijk (2005).

to career-average schemes (pensions based on life-time earnings). Only one in ten active contributors is now making pension contributions under a final pay scheme, compared to one out of two in 2003 (DNB, 2004). Such a change makes the pension funds more actuarially fair, because they henceforth treat more equally members that have received steep salary increases during their career (especially at later stages) and those having had flatter salary profiles, thus avoiding redistribution among contributors. In addition, career-average plans reduce the adverse consequences of salary cuts during the last years of the working life, when productivity tends to decline; such plans induce older workers to accept jobs paying lower salary levels rather than exit to retirement. This shift to career-average plans has been accompanied by other compensatory measures, such as lower deductible and higher pension rates, but the conditionality of indexation clauses means that the shift to career-average schemes is likely to result in lower replacement rates (DNB, 2005). Indeed, many pension funds have provisions allowing them to suspend indexation in case of poor financial performance, thus avoiding the systematic recourse to hikes in contribution rates. As shown in Table 2.2, such a reduction in replacement rates would have a positive effect on long-term budgetary prospects.

Another option to restore the sustainability of public finances is to increase the retirement age embedded in the first pension pillar. Although life expectancy has considerably increased, the standard age of eligibility to a pension has remained fixed at age 65 since the introduction of the current pension system in the post WW2 period. Exacerbating the problem, from the public finance perspective, is the large number of working-age individuals who have prematurely left the workforce under an early retirement plan or the social security plan for long-term disability (WAO). The effective retirement age is estimated to be 61.0 for men and 59.1 for women (see Chapter 3), well below official retirement age of 65. Very few people are thus still in employment when they reach the official retirement age. Hence, like in other countries, pensioners are benefiting from an increasingly long period of inactivity with a pension paid at relatively high replacement rates.

So as to alleviate the burden on public finances, and take advantage of longer, healthier lives, the Dutch pension system should be reformed to discourage early exits from the labour force. Significant increases in labour market participation of older workers have been observed in the past decade, but more needs to be done. Indeed, long-term projections of sustainable public finances assume that the average participation rate will increase by 5 percentage points, which will require an increased labour market mobilisation of older workers. This will not be easily achieved, as early retirement appears to have become a deeply entrenched social choice that may prove difficult to change. Thus, if one early-retirement route is closed, workers may still seek to avail themselves of other routes, such as long-term sick leave or disability insurance benefits. It is therefore important to reform these schemes as well, and the government has put forward proposals to this end. Policy reforms that would contribute to achieving these goals are further discussed in Chapter 3.

Conclusion

The budgetary position has been strengthened at an impressive pace in 2004-05, reversing fiscal slippage that occurred at the start of the decade. Now that this short-term deterioration has been dealt with, the authorities should focus on medium-term sustainability. To begin with, the government should resist pressure for new spending and tax relief that are likely to arise with the emergence of cyclical revenues and natural gas windfalls. The strengthening of the fiscal framework suggested in Box 2.3 could help achieve this goal. In the longer term, despite many enviable features, the pension system poses questions for the sustainability of public finances. Recommendations outlined in the same box are intended to help restore fiscal viability, while contributing to stronger economic performance and improving intergenerational equity.

> ## Box 2.3. **Policy recommendations for returning public finances to a sustainable path**
>
> **Lending coherence to the fiscal framework**
>
> - *Return close to budget balance and aim for a medium-term surplus.* Following the impressive fiscal consolidation in 2004-05, the authorities should resist emerging pressures for renewed spending programmes and tax relief. Revenue windfalls should be used to reduce the deficit, rather than increase spending.
>
> - *Strengthen the fiscal rule.* Even though the "trend-budgeting framework" has well served the purpose of spending restraint, it can be circumvented by creative gimmicks. The authorities should record more comprehensively all tax expenditures and deductions, including for owner occupied housing and pension plans
>
> - *Promote an integrated decision making process.* The strong and sudden increase of available resources for investment that results from higher gas resources should not erode the quality of the investments or the selection process of eligible projects. Therefore, the earmarking of natural gas revenues to special programmes should be subject to close examination.
>
> **Pensions: combining strategies to re-establish sustainability**
>
> - *Pre-fund pension liabilities.* The budget path has deviated from the pre-funding strategy described in 2000, which called for achieving budget surpluses of 1% of GDP. Given past slippages, and weaker financial performance of pension fund investments, re-establishing a general government surplus is important.
>
> - *Encourage later retirement.* The government should continue to encourage later retirement by closing early retirement routes, such as the misuse of disability and unemployment insurance, and reducing the scope of fiscal instruments subsidising early individual retirement strategies. The government should also index the age of eligibility for first-pillar pensions to life expectancy.

Notes

1. The AWBZ contribution was converted into an increase of 0.3% of the first and second income tax band rates.

2. In the CPB (2000) budget simulation of sustainable policy, the stock of public debt falls to a minimum of 8% of GDP by 2040.

3. This deficit partly results from the payment of pension fund contributions above cost-covering levels, which are required to restore the solvency of pension funds. These contributions, which are tax-deductible, temporarily depress government revenues. Notably, employers' contributions were increased from 5.7% of gross salary in 1999 to 10.6% in 2003, reducing corporate income tax receipts correspondingly (DNB, 2004). Once pension fund solvency is restored, contribution rates will return to cost-covering levels and income tax receipts will increase.

4. Persons of 65 and over are exempt from social security contributions, which constitute the largest component of the personal income tax rates, notably in lower and median income brackets.

Bibliography

CPB Netherlands Bureau for Economic Policy Analysis (2000), *Ageing in the Netherlands*, The Hague, SDU Uitgevers and Centraal Planbureau, August.

CPB Netherlands Bureau for Economic Policy Analysis (2003), *The new coalition agreement*, CPB Report 2003/2, The Hague.

CPB (2005a), *Centraal Economisch Plan (CEP) 2005* (Central Economic Plan 2005), Dutch only, The Hague (English summary on institutional changes can be downloaded: *www.cpb.nl/eng/cepmev/cep/2005/ speciale_onderwerpen/stelselwijzigingen_eng.pdf*).

CPB (2005b), *Macro Economische Verkenning 2006* (Macro Economic Outlook 2006), Dutch only, The Hague.

DNB (2004), "Dutch pensions sector: sustainability under pressure", *DNB Quarterly Bulletin*, December 2004.

DNB (2005), "New insight into purchasing power protection for retirees", *DNB Quarterly Bulletin*, June 2005.

EPC (2001), *Budgetary challenges posed by ageing of populations; projected public expenditure on pensions, health and long-term care as well as on education between 2000-2050.*

Girouard, N. and C. André (2005), "Measuring cyclically-adjusted budget balances for OECD countries", *OECD Economics Department Working Paper No. 434.*

Hallerberg, M. Rolf Strauch and J. von Hagen (2004), "The design of fiscal rules and forms of governance in European Union countries", *European Central Bank Working Paper Series*, No. 419, December, Frankfurt.

Kraan, Dirk-Jan (2005), "Typically Dutch", *OECD Journal on Budgeting*, Volume 4, No. 4, Paris.

Ministry of Economic Affairs (2005), *Now for later: energy report 2005*, The Hague.

Ministry of Finance (2005), Budgetmemorandum 2006: main outlines of policy, The Hague.

OECD (2004), *Economic Surveys: Netherlands*, Volume 2004 Issue 9, OECD, Paris.

OECD (2005a), *Netherlands, Ageing and Employment Policies*, Paris.

OECD (2005b), *Trends in International Migration*, Paris.

OECD (2005c), *Pensions at a Glance*, Paris.

Van de Ven, M. (2001), *Ageing, actuarial neutrality and flexible retirement*, CPB Report 2001/3.

Van Ewijk, C. (2005), *Pension Savings and Government Finance in the Netherlands*, OECD Economic Studies, No. 39, 2004/2.

ISBN 92-64-03669-5
OECD Economic Surveys: Netherlands
© OECD 2006

Chapter 3

Labour market reform to increase resilience and labour utilisation

This chapter discusses labour-market reforms to increase macroeconomic resilience and labour utilisation. Strict EPL on regular contracts and long unemployment benefit duration weaken re-equilibrating mechanisms that drive the economy back to trend. Regulations that make EPL strict on regular contracts are identified in the first part of the chapter, along with recent and planned reforms to ease EPL on such contracts and suggestions for further reforms. The need to sharpen incentives for unemployed persons to search for a job early in their unemployment spell is also touched upon. Concerning labour utilisation, the main weaknesses are in female working time and in the employment rate for older workers. Low female working time appears to be mainly attributable to difficulties that mothers have in reconciling family and work life. Childcare and out-of-school-hours care arrangements are being strengthened but more needs to be done. To encourage older workers to remain in the labour force longer, access to publicly subsidised routes to early retirement has progressively been made more difficult but there is still scope to go further, especially in respect of unemployment benefit. At the same time, more needs to be done to enhance the employability of older workers.

As discussed in Chapter 1, relatively strict employment protection legislation (EPL), notably for permanent contracts, and weak incentives for some unemployed persons to search vigorously for a job early in their spell of unemployment, weaken the resilience of the Dutch economy. Strict EPL limits the scope for employers to adjust employment levels to economic conditions, slowing down the market mechanisms that drive an overheating or depressed economy back to trend output. This effect is reinforced when the economy is depressed by weak incentives to search for a job early in an unemployment spell for unemployed persons entitled to benefits for a long duration, lessening the impact of the unemployed on wage formation. While some reforms are planned, more needs to be done to ease EPL and sharpen job search incentives earlier in spells of unemployment. These issues are discussed in the first part of this chapter.

While the Netherlands has made considerable progress since the early 1990s in increasing labour utilisation (defined as total hours worked per member of the working-age population), it remains low by international comparison. Increasing labour utilisation would help to close the gap in GDP *per capita vis-à-vis* the US (see Chapter 1) and, insofar as doing so entailed shifting people off social benefits, would reduce the amount of budget consolidation required to put public finances on a sustainable path. As discussed in Chapter 1, low labour utilisation mainly reflects low working time, especially for women. The other major weakness in labour utilisation is the employment rate of the older working age population which, though above the prevailing EU level, is below the OECD average. The causes of these weaknesses in labour utilisation, reforms underway to attenuate them and suggestions for further reforms are discussed in the remainder of the chapter.

Labour market reforms to increase macroeconomic resilience

Further easing EPL

EPL in the Netherlands is a little stricter than the OECD average (Figure 3.1). This reflects very strict EPL on regular contracts, low EPL on temporary contracts and additional requirements for collective dismissals that are around the average. The main feature that makes EPL on regular contracts strict by international comparison is high procedural inconveniences for dismissing a worker (Table 3.1). This reflects a long delay before the start of the notice period (31 days compared with an OECD average of 10 days) and cumbersome procedures to be followed – the labour authority (Centres for Work and Income, CWI) must be notified if the employee objects. The difficulty of dismissal is also high by international comparison. In addition, compensation for unfair dismissal is high, rising to 18 months pay after 20 years of tenure compared with an OECD average of 12 months. Regulation in the remaining category underlying the overall summary EPL indicator – notice and severance pay for no-fault individual dismissals – is only slightly stricter than the OECD average. This reflects relatively short notice periods but high severance pay for dismissed employees with long tenure (9 months of pay after 20 years of tenure compared with an OECD average of 3 months) (OECD, 2004, Annex 1.A2).

Figure 3.1. **Overall strictness of EPL in 2003**

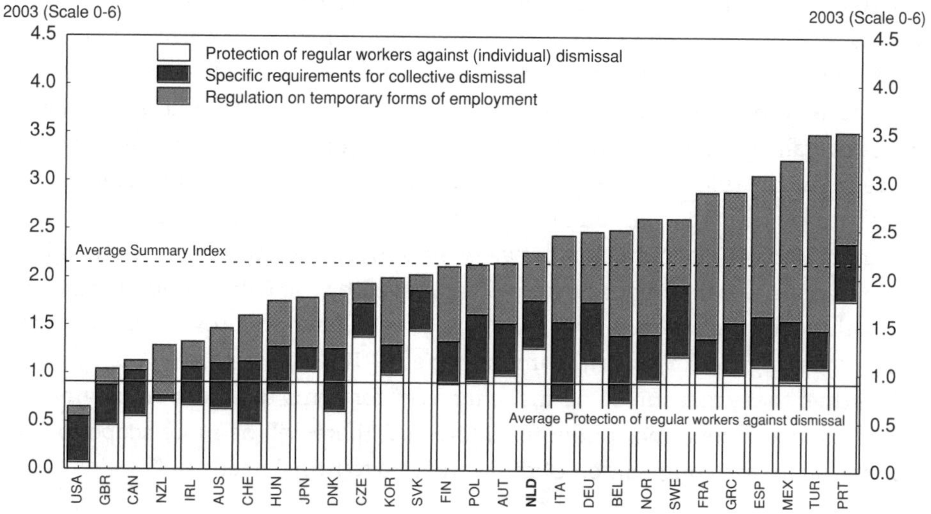

Source: OECD (2004a), OECD Employment Outlook.

Table 3.1. **Indicators of the strictness of employment protection for regular employment**[1]

	Regular procedural inconveniences			Notice and severance pay for no-fault individual dismissals			Difficulty of dismissal			Overall strictness of protection against dismissals		
	Late 1980s	Late 1990s	2003	Late 1980s	Late 1990s	2003	Late 1980s	Late 1990s	2003	Late 1980s	Late 1990s	2003
Australia	0.5	1.5	1.5	1.0	1.0	1.0	1.5	2.0	2.0	1.0	1.5	1.5
Austria	2.5	2.5	2.5	2.0	2.0	0.9	4.3	4.3	3.8	2.9	2.9	2.4
Belgium	1.0	1.0	1.0	2.3	2.3	2.4	1.8	1.8	1.8	1.7	1.7	1.7
Canada	1.0	1.0	1.0	1.0	1.0	1.0	2.0	2.0	2.0	1.3	1.3	1.3
Czech Republic	–	3.5	3.5	–	2.7	2.7	–	3.8	3.8	–	3.3	3.3
Denmark	1.0	1.0	1.0	2.0	1.9	1.9	1.5	1.5	1.5	1.5	1.5	1.5
Finland	4.8	2.8	2.8	1.9	1.4	1.0	1.8	2.8	2.8	2.8	2.3	2.2
France	2.5	2.5	2.5	1.5	1.5	1.9	3.0	3.0	3.0	2.3	2.3	2.5
Germany	3.5	3.5	3.5	1.0	1.3	1.3	3.3	3.3	3.3	2.6	2.7	2.7
Greece	2.0	2.0	2.0	2.4	2.2	2.2	3.0	2.8	3.0	2.5	2.3	2.4
Hungary	–	1.5	1.5	–	1.8	1.8	–	2.5	2.5	–	1.9	1.9
Ireland	2.0	2.0	2.0	0.8	0.8	0.8	2.0	2.0	2.0	1.6	1.6	1.6
Italy	1.5	1.5	1.5	0.6	0.6	0.6	3.3	3.3	3.3	1.8	1.8	1.8
Japan	2.0	2.0	2.0	1.8	1.8	1.8	3.3	3.5	3.5	2.4	2.4	2.4
Korea	–	3.3	3.3	–	0.9	0.9	–	3.0	3.0	–	2.4	2.4
Mexico	–	1.0	1.0	–	2.1	2.1	–	3.7	3.7	–	2.3	2.3
Netherlands	**5.5**	**4.0**	**4.0**	**1.0**	**1.9**	**1.9**	**2.8**	**3.3**	**3.3**	**3.1**	**3.1**	**3.1**
New Zealand	1.3	1.3	2.0	–	0.4	0.4	–	2.3	2.7	–	1.4	1.7
Norway	2.0	2.0	2.0	1.0	1.0	1.0	3.8	3.8	3.8	2.3	2.3	2.3
Poland	–	3.0	3.0	–	1.4	1.4	–	2.3	2.3	–	2.2	2.2
Portugal	4.0	3.5	3.5	5.0	5.0	5.0	5.5	4.5	4.0	4.8	4.3	4.2
Slovak Republic	–	5.0	5.0	–	2.7	2.7	–	3.3	2.8	–	3.6	3.5
Spain	4.8	2.0	2.0	3.1	2.6	2.6	3.8	3.3	3.3	3.9	2.6	2.6
Sweden	3.0	3.0	3.0	1.7	1.6	1.6	4.0	4.0	4.0	2.9	2.9	2.9
Switzerland	0.5	0.5	0.5	1.5	1.5	1.5	1.5	1.5	1.5	1.2	1.2	1.2
Turkey	2.0	2.0	2.0	–	3.4	3.4	–	2.5	2.3	–	2.6	2.6
United Kingdom	1.0	1.0	1.0	1.1	1.0	1.1	0.8	0.8	1.3	0.9	0.9	1.1
United States	0.0	0.0	0.0	0.0	0.0	0.0	0.5	0.5	0.5	0.2	0.2	0.2
Average	2.2	2.2	2.2	2.5	1.9	1.8	3.0	3.0	3.0	2.3	2.0	2.0

–: Data not available.

1. See OECD (2004a), OECD Employment Outlook, Chapter 2, for a detailed description of employment protection regulation and Annex 2.A.1 for the scoring methodology.

Source: OECD (2004a), OECD Employment Outlook.

The government recently announced measures that come into effect in October 2006 to ease EPL on regular contracts (see Box 3.1 for a brief description of the Dutch dismissal process). The LIFO (last-in-first-out) principle for selecting employees to be laid off as a result of poor business conditions, which protects older workers more than others, is to be replaced by the "reflection" principle, whereby workers are selected to mirror the overall age composition of the firm's employees.[1] In addition, firms will be able to deviate from this rule in agreement with unions, applying their own criteria to decide which staff to lay off. This will make it possible to target employees with relatively weak performance. Moreover, agreements between employers and employees on dismissals for economic reasons will no longer have to be approved by the CWI. Another feature of the reform is that dismissed employees will no longer have to prove that they resisted dismissal to be eligible for unemployment benefit (UB), reducing administrative costs.[2] Taken together, these measures will make it easier for firms to adjust employment levels in response to poor economic conditions. Moreover, there will be more scope to use such occasions to adapt the composition of the workforce to firms' needs.

Box 3.1. **The dual system in the Dutch dismissal process**

In the Netherlands, there are two channels for terminating employment contracts – via the Labour Office (CWI) or third-party intermediation from a local court. If termination occurs via the CWI, the procedure has to fulfill a number of criteria (last-in first-out principle, non-discriminatory composition of the list of persons, etc.) and must be based on sufficiently important reasons (such as no work whatsoever available in the firm and incapability unless caused by illness) to obtain the necessary consent from dismissal advisory boards, consisting of employers' organisations and unions. On the other hand, there is no severance pay. Termination via third-party intermediation from local court is faster as it limits the number of parties involved in the conflict and has increased greatly during the 1990s. However, this procedure is more expensive, as the judge's severance pay formula, by which most cases are settled, generally provides for one month of salary per year of service, which the judge may deviate from according to the circumstances of the case.*

* In November 2000, an advisory commission to the government recommended to abolish the administrative route altogether, keeping only the court route. This recommendation triggered an explicit demand by the social partners to keep the current dual system.

Nevertheless, most of the features that make EPL on regular contracts strict in the Netherlands remain in place; the only indicator underpinning strict EPL discussed above that changes as a result of these reforms is that procedural inconveniences are slightly lower as it is no longer necessary to get the approval of the CWI for a dismissal for economic reasons. Reducing EPL further would entail easing regulations on the remaining items that make it relatively strict or giving firms still greater flexibility to resort to temporary employment contracts, notably by increasing the maximum permissible number of successive contracts (it is presently 3, although the social partners can agree to allow more, whereas there is no limit in a number of other countries).

Progressively reducing unemployment benefit replacement rates as duration rises

Based on international experience, search activity by unemployed persons tends to spike around the time that benefits are expected to decrease (Holmlund, 1998). Hence, shortening the interval before benefits begin to decline would increase the impact of the unemployed on wage developments, strengthening the economy's re-equilibrating mechanisms. While the planned reduction in the maximum duration of UB to 38 months will help to curtail its use as a pathway to early retirement (see below), the still long duration of UB is likely to continue to delay the reaction of wage rates to developments in unemployment. In the event that this delay continues to be a problem, the social partners and the government should consider progressively reducing the UB replacement rate part way through the benefit entitlement period so that UB smoothly converges to the social assistance level by the time that UB entitlements expire.

Increasing working time

As noted in Chapter 1, short average working time mainly reflects the high proportion of women that work part-time (defined as normal working time of less than 30 hours per week). In addition, working time for full-time employees is low – relatively few men or women work 40 hours or more per week. The concentration of short working time among women might point to difficulties in reconciling work and family life. High marginal tax rates on second earners' incomes may also be a factor. Concerning the relatively short working time for full-time employees, collective agreements aimed at sharing work around may have contributed to this outcome.

Reducing costs to parents of childcare and out-of-school hours care would encourage mothers to work longer hours

While considerable progress has been made in increasing the availability of childcare facilities – the number of such facilities, which used to be one of the lowest in the European Union (OECD, 2001, p. 144), has doubled since 1998 – the cost, quality and availability of such facilities has continued to be a barrier to increasing female working time. In order to enhance access to good quality childcare, the government passed a new Childcare Act that came into effect in January 2005. Under the new law, the government sets national quality standards and subsidies are paid to parents instead of suppliers, increasing competitive pressures in the sector (parents can more easily vote with their feet). The government pays a subsidy that amounts on average to FRACTION1/3 of childcare costs. Employers are expected on average to pay a further of childcare costs, with the remainder to be paid by parents. In the event that employers do not pay their share, the government covers their contribution; presently, 73.5% of employers pay their share of childcare costs and this proportion is expected to reach 90% by 2008. The government subsidy is phased down as household annual income rises above 130% of the minimum wage, reaching zero at € 74 000. The subsidy to cover unpaid employer contributions is also progressively withdrawn as household income rises above 130% of the minimum wage, but the taper rate is higher, so that this subsidy falls to zero at € 45 000.

The introduction of the Childcare Act has benefited low-income families. However, many middle-income families have found that their net childcare costs have increased significantly as they receive little or no subsidy, are no longer able to claim a tax deduction and in some cases no longer benefit from employer support. As a result, some middle-income families may reduce the intensity of childcare participation or consider stopping using formal childcare, with adverse consequences for female working time. Indeed, complaints have been made that childcare participation has decreased (e.g., by the labour union FNV), although part of this reduction may have been caused by the economic downturn. Faced with a fall in demand, many childcare providers have cut back capacity. In response to these developments, the government recently announced an increase in the budget for childcare subsidies of € 130 million from 2006, taking the total budget to some € 1.1 billion. This money is to be used to lower the taper rate for the withdrawal of childcare subsidies such that they will fall to zero only when household annual income reaches € 96 000. Even after the reform, the share of childcare costs paid by parents rises rapidly as household income increases from around € 1 500 per month to € 7 000, especially if employers don't pay their share (Figure 3.2). The child care financing system will be evaluated in 2006. If the findings lead to the conclusion that further steps are needed, further reductions in the taper rate at which subsidies are withdrawn (including the government subsidy for unpaid employer contributions) should be considered. In this context, it would be necessary to take steps to counter the possible negative effect of an increase in government subsidies on employers' contributions.

Figure 3.2. **Shares of childcare costs paid by employees, employers and government by income level**[1, 2]

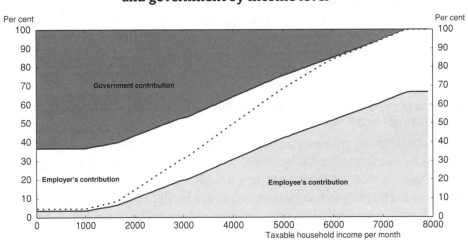

1. Assumptions: one child, childcare costs per hour = 5.60 euro
2. Half of the increase in the childcare budget (i.e., 100 million euro) decided on in August 2005 has been included in the figure.

Source: CPB (2005), *Macro Economische Verkenning 2006* (Macro Economic Outlook 2006), Dutch only, The Hague.

A lack of affordable out-of-school hours (OSH) care is also a barrier to increased working time by mothers. This problem is accentuated by the facts that children are in general sent home at lunchtime and on Wednesday afternoons. In addition, school days may be shortened or cancelled when teachers take sick leave or their extra holidays (*ADV-dagen*)[3] that must be taken at relatively short notice (they cannot be cumulated) owing to a lack of replacement teachers. Indeed, 35% of all schools occasionally send children home (resulting in the loss of 2% of the school year in these schools), rising to more than 50% for inner city schools (based on the academic year 2000-2001, van Langen and Hulsen, 2001); although this situation has improved in recent years due to a decline in sickness leave and an increase in the number of substitute teachers. In order to address these problems, the government is promoting a "chain-arrangement" with an all day supply of OSH care in co-operation with local actors. The programme aims at strengthening local chains of institutions and provisions in the period 2005-2007 in at least 100 municipalities and extending such arrangements to at least 1 200 schools by 2010. As a first step, the government made € 70 million available to support such arrangements in the 2006 Budget. Moreover, the government has accepted a Parliament resolution requiring all schools to provide pre- and after-school care facilities (between 8.30 and 18.30) if parents ask for them. OSH care is likely to be highly cost effective – the per student costs are relatively low, certainly much lower than childcare costs,[4] and mothers are freed from many hours of care responsibilities, making it easier to increase hours worked if so desired. The government should provide more support for such arrangements to relieve this constraint on increasing working time. It should also ensure that replacement teachers are available so that children are not sent home for lack of a teacher and negotiate the termination of the extra holidays for teachers that must be taken at short notice. In the Netherlands, schools themselves are responsible for finding replacement teachers. The salary costs for these replacement teachers are compensated through the Substitution Fund (*Vervangingsfonds*), making it easier for schools to replace teachers on sick leave. The government should also work with employers and unions to reduce teacher sick-leave absences, which are high relative to those in other professions. In the last five years great steps have been taken in this respect. Because of agreements on work conditions, so-called labour-covenants (*Arbo-convenanten*), teacher sick leave has dropped by 30% between 2000 and 2004.

Lowering marginal effective tax rates would increase incentives to work longer hours

Even abstracting from the effect of progressively withdrawing childcare subsidies as household income rises, marginal effective tax rates for second-earners switching from part-time to full-time employment in low-income households are high owing to the withdrawal of income-related benefits (such as tax credits for households with children, individual rent subsidies, and subsidies for the education costs of children) (Table 3.2). This problem has been partly mitigated by increases in the earned income tax credit, the combination credit (tax credit for people who work and have children) and the additional combination credit (for employees in low income households and single parents).

Table 3.2. **Marginal effective tax rates for second earner part-time employees, 2002**[1]

Per cent

Woman switches from	½ to full		⅓ to full		⅔ to full	
	No children	Two children	No children	Two children	No children	Two children
Austria	40	40	28	28	41	41
Belgium	57	57	51	51	55	55
Czech Republic	28	27	26	24	28	27
Germany	51	52	51	51	52	52
Denmark	48	48	44	44	50	50
Finland	42	42	33	33	44	44
France	37	30	29	22	38	32
Italy	38	44	35	46	41	46
Japan	21	27	21	21	21	30
Netherlands	**45**	**56**	**37**	**37**	**46**	**46**
Norway	34	34	33	33	36	36
Sweden	35	35	31	34	35	35
United Kingdom	32	32	32	26	32	32
United States	28	26	25	17	29	29
Average	38	39	34	33	39	40

1. The head of household works full-time and earns 67% of average gross wages in the relevant country. Children are aged 4 and 6. Changes in rent subsidies and tax credits, etc., are taken into account. The withdrawal of childcare subsidies is not taken into account.

Source: OECD (2004b), *Benefits and Wages: OECD Indicators.*

Marginal effective tax rates are particularly high for sole earner households with children and earnings below twice the model income and spike at the modal income (Table 3.3). For such households, net income decreases when gross income reaches the modal income as they lose a tax credit for households with children in one hit. The recent increase in this marginal effective tax rate is the consequence of the rise in this tax credit in 2005. To eliminate the inactivity trap just below modal income, the government intends to integrate the various tax credits for people with children and to phase them out from the modal income at a taper rate of 6%. In addition, the government has reduced the taper rate for withdrawing childcare subsidies (see above) and rendered the school-fee subsidy for lower income households redundant by abolishing tuition fees for children below the school-leaving age. Furthermore, Parliament has requested the Ministry of Housing, Spatial Planning and the Environment to look at the modalities of changing individual rent subsidies to reduce marginal effective tax rates.

Table 3.3. **Marginal effective tax rates (low-wage trap)**[1]

In per cent

	Level 2003	Level 2004	Level 2005
2 adults, 1 income, with child(ren)			
Minimum plus	92	75	76
Modal income	123	122	139
Twice modal income	55	55	55
2 adults, 2 incomes, with child(ren), income of lowest earner rises			
Minimum plus + half minimum plus	26	36	36
Modal income + half modal income	34	33	33
Twice modal income + modal income	46	47	49

1. The marginal pressure for a single earner with children and a modal income leads to a net decrease in income when the gross income rises. This is because the group just before modal income still benefits from an additional tax credit for people with children whereas this tax credit is fully withdrawn at the modal income. The increase in marginal pressure therefore is the consequence of the rise in this tax credit in 2005. The Cabinet intends to implement a gradual phasing out of these arrangements as of 2006. These calculations do not take into account the progressive withdrawal of childcare subsidies as household income rises above 130% of the minimum wage.

Source: Ministry of Social Affairs and Employment.

Budget room for extra expenditure on care subsidies and cuts in marginal effective tax rates could be made by phasing out tax subsidies on owner-occupied housing

Budget room for increased expenditure on subsidies for childcare and OSH care could be found by phasing out tax subsidies for owner-occupied housing, for which there is a strong case (OECD, 2004a, pp. 47-57). Personal income tax deductions for mortgage interest payments by owner-occupiers amount to € 8.8 billion (2004), representing about one-third of personal income tax receipts, although part of the budget savings from phasing out such tax deductions would need to be used to reduce relatively high property taxes and imputed rental payments which are estimated by the authorities to claw back 50-60% of these tax deductions. Such a move would build on the steps that the government has already taken in this regard. Since 2001, it has placed a ceiling (30 years) on the period during which interest payments can be deducted from personal income, limited tax deductibility to the principal residence and, for owner-occupiers moving house, to interest on that part of the mortgage that is equal to the home's purchase price less equity withdrawal from the previous home. The Dutch government does not plan to implement any further such reforms during the remainder of its current term in office (until 2007).

Social partners could also contribute to increasing working time by making it a priority

There is evidence (Alesina, Glaeser and Sacerdote, 2005) that suggests that the large reduction in working time in European countries relative to that in most other OECD countries, including the United States, can be explained partly by the activities of unions, which in Europe have tried to defend membership in the face of shocks through work sharing (*i.e.*, reducing the number of hours worked per employee). In the Netherlands, in the face of high unemployment during the 1980s, the social partners agreed to reduce the standard full-time working week from 40 hours to only 36 hours. The social partners could contribute to extending working time by agreeing lower overtime premiums. This would make it more attractive for employers to offer longer working time, increasing opportunities for employees wishing to work longer to earn more to do so, thereby, allowing a greater freedom in the choice between remunerated work and leisure time. At the same time, employees who do not want to work longer would not be obliged to do so.

Raising employment rates of older workers

Since breaking with the policy following the first- and second oil shocks of encouraging older workers to retire early to make way for younger workers, the Dutch authorities have reversed the decline in employment rates that this policy had caused: the employment rate for older workers has risen from a low of 25% in 1986 to 44% in 2003, the same rate as before the first oil shock in 1973. Nevertheless, this employment rate remains low by international comparison (see Chapter 1, Figure 1.8) as does the effective retirement age of 61.0 for men and 59.1 for women (Figure 3.3). This section discusses recent and planned measures to increase the employment rate for older workers further and suggests areas where reforms should be taken further.

Closing exit routes to early retirement and indexing the official retirement age to life expectancy

There are a variety of publicly subsidised arrangements that provide pathways to early retirement. The most important are: disability benefit (DB), which was received by 13% of the population aged 50-64 in 2002; early retirement schemes, from which 6% of persons in this age group benefited; and UB and social assistance (SA), each of which was paid to 3% of persons in this age group (OECD, 2005a, p. 11). The government is making considerable progress in restricting access to these routes to early retirement.

Curtailing access to the disability benefit pathway to early retirement

The large stock of older DB recipients partly reflects past misuse of the scheme as a route to early retirement – following reforms since the early 1990s, there is now much less such misuse. To discourage the use of DB as a dismissal device, employers have had to pay more for the mandatory sick-pay period that precedes application for a DB since 1996. The law obliges them to pay at least 70% of the salary for the first year of sickness. However, most employers pay 100%. The sick-pay period (at the employer's charge) was extended to two years from 1 January 2004, and employers were encouraged by the government not to pay more than 70% in the second year of illness. Another measure to discourage use of DB for workforce management was the introduction in 1998 of experience rating of disability insurance premiums paid by employers, known as the PEMBA scheme. To reduce the adverse effect that this measure could have on incentives to hire older persons, employers have been exempt from paying the fixed part of the disability insurance contribution for

Figure 3.3. **Average effective and official age of retirement in OECD countries, 1997-2002**[1]

Percentages of each age group

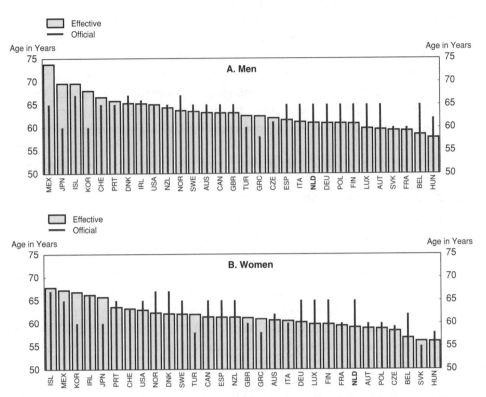

1. The average effective age of retirement is derived from the observed decline in participation rates over a five-year period for successive cohorts of workers (by five-year age groups) aged 40 and over.

Source: OECD estimates derived from the European Labour Force Survey and national labour force surveys.

employees aged 55 years or over and for all new hires aged 50 or over (subject to a break of at least 6 months where a previous employment relationship is being renewed). Finally, screening of DB applicants was reinforced under the 2002 Gatekeeper Act, which introduced stricter mutual obligations on long-term sickness benefit recipients and their employers. These measures together reduced the number of inflows by one-quarter in 2003, reflecting a decline in sickness benefit take-up in 2002 that continued in 2003.

The government and the social partners have agreed a major reform to disability insurance that comes into effect in January 2006. It is aimed at permanently reducing annual inflows into the scheme to 25 000 (from 70 000 – 100 000 per year in the past decade) and at strengthening incentives for the partially disabled to use their remaining work capacity fully (see *ibid.*, Box 3.6 for a description of the reform). Eligibility criteria are being substantially tightened: full disability will entail that recovery is medically impossible or that after two years of disability it has become evident that recovery can not be expected for a longer period of time. With the extension of the sick-pay period in January 2004, DB applicants have been cut to almost nothing in 2005,[5] creating capacity to retest the existing stock of DB recipients using the new, stricter criteria. In the first nine months of this procedure, 55 000 people on DB have been re-evaluated (out of a total of 326 000 beneficiaries) and 35% of benefits were either ended or reduced (UWV, 2005). This ratio is likely to fall, however, as retesting continues because it started with younger disabled persons. A major weakness in re-evaluation of the stock of DB recipients is that it only concerns beneficiaries aged less than 50.

Reducing the scope to use unemployment-related benefits as pathways to early retirement

A number of measures have been taken to restrict use of UB as a pathway to early retirement. First, the second-stage benefit (providing up to 70% of the minimum wage for 2 to 3.5 years) available to unemployed persons aged 57½ or over who have exhausted their entitlement to UB was abolished on 1 January 2004 for persons who have become unemployed on or after 11 August 2003.[6] Second, age was removed from the criteria determining UB duration in January 2005, although the long transition phase until age no longer affects duration at all means that the impact of this measure will be limited for some time to come.[7] At the end of this transition phase, duration will only depend on the unemployed person's work history. Third, job search obligations were re-instated on 1 January 2004 for unemployed persons on benefits aged 57½ years or older, although there are a number of exemptions.[8] It will be necessary to monitor these exemptions to ensure that they do not undermine the intent of the reform.

Moreover, the social partners and the government have agreed a major UB reform that comes into effect in October 2006 (see *ibid.*, Box 3.7 for a summary of the main measures). The main feature of the reform that concerns older workers is that the maximum duration of UB is to be cut from 5 years to 38 months. While this represents significant progress, the shortened duration limit nevertheless remains high by international comparison (see OECD, 1999, Table 2.2). The reform also introduces a non-income related benefit at welfare level after rights to UB are exhausted. This benefit will be exempt from an assets means test for persons aged 50 or over and will also be exempt from a partner income test for persons aged 60 or over. Such a benefit instead of social assistance weakens incentives for beneficiaries to find a job.

The government has also proposed to base UB entitlements for persons aged 55 or more at the date of dismissal on their highest previous salary in cases of multiple spells of unemployment. This is a promising measure to reduce a potential barrier to older unemployed persons accepting a lower-paid job than before that deserves social partners' support. The government is also considering options to attenuate the possible impact on dismissals of older workers of the replacement of the LIFO principle in redundancies with the "reflection" principle (see above), which reduce protection for older workers to the same level as for other workers. One option could be to introduce experience rating for employers' UB contributions for older workers (aged 55 or over) with, for example, an exemption for workers employed when they were already aged 50 or more. However, this could be a retrograde step, as it would compromise the progress that has been made towards age-neutrality in rules for collective dismissals. Moreover, it could backfire as has occurred in other countries (Austria and France[9]) that have sought to penalise employers laying off older workers by encouraging employers to make workers redundant before they reach the age at which the penalties apply (55 years of age in this proposal) and/or not to hire workers approaching the age at which new hires are exempt (50 years of age in this proposal).

Terminating tax incentives for early retirement schemes

Early retirement schemes (VUT) were introduced in the late 1970s to encourage older workers to retire early so as to make employment room for younger workers. They were financed on a PAYG basis through a levy on the gross wage bill and operated on a sectoral basis. These schemes proved very popular, with the number of beneficiaries rising from 20 000 in the early 1980s to 150 000 in the early 1990s. Following the 1997 Pension Covenant, the social partners rapidly replaced VUT with funded pre-pension schemes.[10] As these schemes and occupational pension schemes (which generally have flexible retirement ages) operate on a more actuarially fair basis, this change led to a massive reduction in the incidence of early retirement on VUT, pre-pension or occupational pension schemes (OECD, 2005, Figures 3.3). To reduce incentives further to use VUT or pre-pension schemes, tax incentives for them will be terminated as from January 2006. Employees that have participated in (funded) pre-pension schemes will be able to add these funds to their regular old-age pensions or to the newly created life-course savings scheme, which receives the same tax treatment (EET) as the pre-pension scheme did.[11] Given the fact that the new life-course savings scheme can be used as an individual early retirement scheme,[12] the new scheme may partially offset the impact on early retirement of the termination of tax subsidies for funded collective early retirement schemes. The impact of the termination of these tax subsidies could also be compromised if the remaining scope to build up higher levels of (tax facilitated) collective old-age pension entitlements were used, as they can be used to finance early retirement under the condition of full actuarial neutrality.

Indexing the official retirement age to life expectancy

As discussed in Chapter 2, rising life expectancy is extending the duration of retirement, increasing pension and healthcare costs of the elderly. When current pension arrangements were set up in the post World War II period, retirement was relatively short, especially in relation to working lives. Despite the large increase in life expectancy, especially at older ages, the official retirement age has remained fixed at 65 owing to the unpopularity of increasing it. One approach that could de-politicise this issue and be accepted as a reasonable solution would be to index the official retirement age to life expectancy at that age, as is now done in Germany and France (where the pressure to act has been stronger owing to the greater importance of public pensions in the absence of substantial pre-funded second pillar arrangements). Such a measure should be complemented by applying a similar condition to the minimum age at which flexible retirement can be taken in occupational pension schemes.[13]

Strengthening the employability of older workers through increased training

While participation of older (aged 50-64 years) workers and unemployed persons in training programmes is above the OECD average, it is far below that in the best-performing European countries (Figure 3.4). Moreover, the gap in training participation between older persons and others is particularly large. In part, this large gap can be attributed to the high proportion of low-skilled (i.e., education attainment below the upper secondary level) women in the older age group relative to the younger age group (Table 3.4): research indicates that people who have not completed upper secondary education take part in enterprise training to a lesser extent (ibid., p. 116). As the current generation of older workers is replaced by younger cohorts with fewer school drop outs, this problem will fade,

Figure 3.4. **Participation in training in selected European countries, 2003**[1]

Percentages of each age group

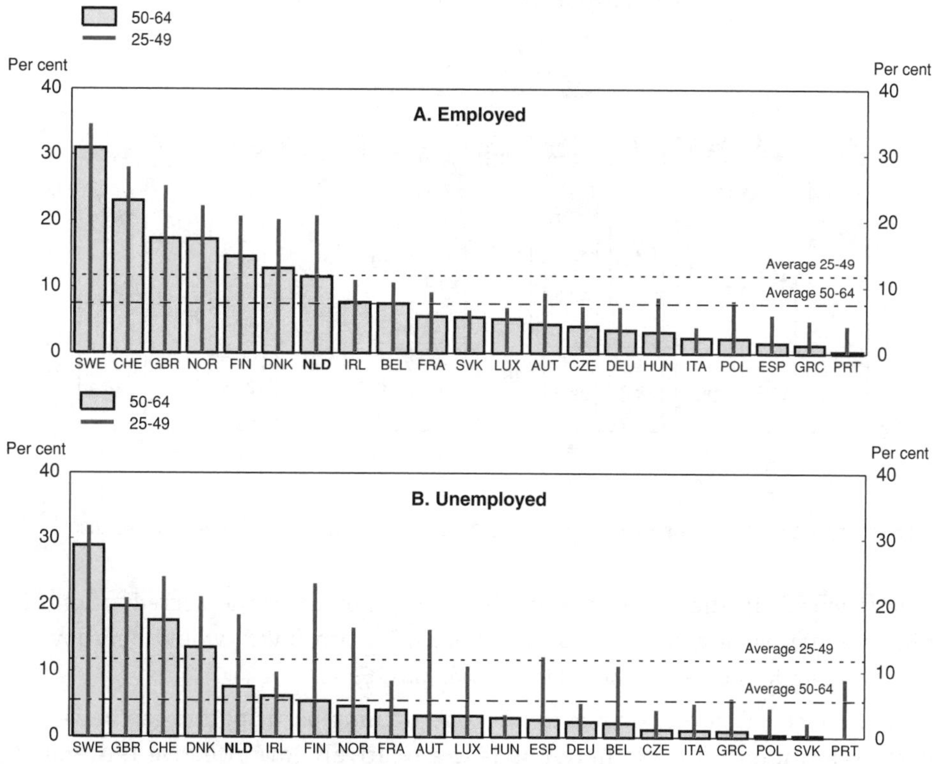

1. Unweighted averages of all countries excluding Switzerland and Norway.

Source: OECD AFA, FATS and STAN databases.

Table 3.4. **Low-skilled population in selected OECD countries by age and gender, 2002**[1]

In per cent

	25-49		50-64	
	Men	Women	Men	Women
NLD	**27.7**	**29.1**	**35.3**	**53.5**
CHE	11.4	14.4	15.7	25.4
DEU	12.1	16.6	13.0	26.9
SWE	13.9	10.6	31.1	26.7
UK	10.8	14.3	21.9	30.2
USA	13.2	10.8	14.1	14.3
EU-19	26.1	27.3	38.5	50.1
OECD	28.9	30.3	38.3	44.5

1. Low skilled is defined as less than upper secondary education attainment.

Source: OECD (2005b), *Education at a Glance.*

reducing the gap in training participation between older and younger workers. Nevertheless, the proportion of older workers not having completed upper secondary education is likely to remain high by international comparison, holding back training participation (Figure 3.5). The long-term solution to this problem is to reduce the proportion of students that leaves formal education before having completed upper

Figure 3.5. **Education level of older workers in selected OECD countries, 2000 and 2025**

Percentage shares of labour force aged 50-64

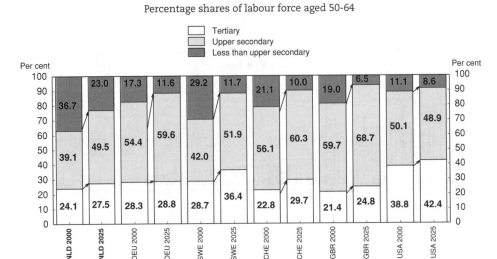

Source: For 2000, OECD (2002), *Education at a Glance*; for 2025, OECD estimates based on the data for 2000.

secondary school. In the meantime, further development of the accreditation of prior learning, validation of experience and skill certification (EVC), would help low-skilled workers to upgrade their educational level (*ibid.*, p. 116).

Another factor that contributes to the large training participation gap between older workers and others in the Netherlands is the relatively low effective retirement age, reducing the time available to amortise training investments (see Figure 3.3). As the various measures to make working longer take effect, this factor will also become a less negative influence on training participation of older workers. Even so, the short payback period will remain an obstacle, as in other countries. This suggests that it may be more attractive to increase training investments in the mid-career (aged 35-50) age group, thereby increasing the employability of future generations of older workers and the return on investing in more training for them (*ibid.*, p. 17). The new life-course-savings scheme offers opportunities in this respect.

> **Box 3.2. Policy recommendations for easing EPL and increasing labour stabilisation**
>
> **Ease EPL**
>
> The government should ease strict EPL on regular contracts to increase macroeconomic resilience and raise employment among groups with low participation rates by:
>
> - Further simplifying dismissal procedures;
> - Widening the circumstances in which a dismissal is justified; and
> - Reducing severance pay obligations for dismissed employees with long tenure.
>
> **Lengthen working hours**
>
> To increase working time, the government should:
>
> - Consider further reducing the taper rate for withdrawing childcare subsidies as household income rises, subject to findings of the evaluation in 2006 of the child care financing system;
> - Increase subsidies for out-of-school hours care, as is being considered;
> - Require schools to make arrangements so that children are not sent home when teachers are absent;
> - Go further in reducing high marginal effective tax rates associated with the withdrawal of household income related benefits by withdrawing individual rent subsidies more slowly; and
> - Encourage the social partners to reduce overtime wage premiums.
>
> **Raise older workers participation**
>
> To increase the employment rate for older workers, the government should:
>
> - Closely monitor the impact of the reform of the UB-scheme on its use as an exit-route to early retirement. Even after the reform, the maximum duration of the benefit is relatively long compared with other countries, where duration of 1-2 years is more usual;
> - Monitor the use of the new individual life course savings scheme and prevent it from becoming an alternative route to early retirement;
> - Index the future official retirement age to life expectancy and encourage social partners to make concomitant adjustments to the age at which (actuarially fair) early retirement can be taken in occupational pension schemes; and
> - Promote the employability of older workers by encouraging greater participation in lifelong learning, especially at mid-career ages (35-50).

Notes

1. It is already possible to apply the reflection principle instead of LIFO; however, the CWI noted recently that only one-sixth of employees involved in collective dismissal of 20 or more are selected based on this principle (OECD, 2005).

2. This measure is expected to save the government € 100 million per year in administrative costs.

3. These holidays were introduced in the 1980s to help absorb a surplus of teachers. However, these extra holidays ("ADV") are not exclusive to the education sector. In the education field these extra holidays are used to compensate the long working week during the regular school year in order to regulate the hours necessary for the regular vacations.

4. For example, it would cost far less to hire a student to mind 15 10-year olds in a sports hall at school than to employ a professional carer for four 2-year olds.

5. This inflow has not dropped to zero, however, because in a limited number of obvious cases (persons with a full disability having reached a stable condition and having no chance of recovery) entry into DB will be possible before the end of the sick-pay period.

6. This benefit was neither income-means nor capital-means tested.

7. Work history will be counted from 1998 onwards. For earlier periods, the old arrangements, which take into account both work history and age, will continue to apply.

8. These include: persons aged 64 on the first day of unemployment; those who moved from DB to UB and were aged 57½ years or more on 31 January 2003 (thus, the exemption will expire in July 2010); those unemployed for less than one year engaged in voluntary work (usually caring for family members) and aged 57½ years or more on 31 December 2003 (thus, the exemption will expire in July 2010); those unemployed for more than one year; and those whom the employment services or municipalities deem to have little or no chance of finding a job.

9. The negative effect of this measure (introduced in 1987) on employment of older workers in France occurred despite additional subsidies designed to reduce their non-wage labour costs.

10. . VUT schemes are now available to only 2% of all employees with transition to the new schemes expected to expire by 2015 (OECD, 2005, p. 64-65).

11. Employees are allowed to save up to 12% of gross yearly income and to cumulate maximum savings of 210% of yearly income.

12. The primary aims are to enable workers to achieve a better balance between work and private life and to maintain their human capital.

13. Even in the absence of such a measure, the age at which flexible pensions are taken would tend to rise because such pensions would be lower at any age before the official retirement age owing to the longer interval before first-pillar pension is paid.

Bibliography

Alesina, A., E. L. Glaeser and B. Sacerdote (2005), "Work and Leisure in the US and Europe: Why So Different?", NBER Working Paper 11278.

CPB (2005), Macro Economische Verkenning 2006 (Macro Economic Outlook 2006), The Hague.

DNB (2005), Quarterly Bulletin, March.

Eurostat (2001), "European Labour Force Survey", Luxembourg.

Holmlund, B. (1998), "Unemployment Insurance in Theory and Practice,"Scandinavian Journal of Economics 100, pp. 113-141.

Langen, A. van and Hulsen, M. (2001), Schooltijden in het Basisonderwijs: Feiten en Fictie (School Hours in Primary Education: Facts and Fiction), Dutch only, ITS, Nijmegen.

OECD (1999), Benefit Systems and Work Incentives, Paris.

OECD(2002), OECD Education at a Glance, Paris.

OECD (2004a), Employment Outlook, Paris.

OECD (2004b), Benefits and Wages: OECD Indicators, Paris.

OECD (2005a), Ageing and Employment Policies – Netherlands, Paris.

OECD (2005b), Education at a Glance, Paris.

UWV (2005), UWV 2e kwartaal 2005 (UWV 2nd quarter 2005).

ISBN 92-64-03669-5
OECD Economic Surveys: Netherlands
© OECD 2006

Chapter 4

Further improvement
of product market competition,
especially in services

This chapter discusses options for further product market reform, especially in services, so as to increase productivity growth. It identifies the main regulatory barriers to product market competition based notably on the OECD Product Market Regulation database. Reducing the barriers to entrepreneurship prevailing in the Netherlands – in particular, the licence and permit procedures – and preventing distortions from state control are important to foster competition and productivity growth. The chapter notably sheds light on the barriers in the distribution and finance sectors, which appear to have hindered the profitable use of ICT in these sectors. Competition seems to be weak in the Dutch retail sector due to strict regulations that limit entry of (large) stores and restrict shop opening hours. As well, the lack of integration of the retail financial market across the European Union seems to be an important obstacle to productivity growth in the financial sector.

Introduction

Product market competition tends to strengthen productivity growth. Competition between existing firms, entry of new and foreign firms and the threat of entry enhance the efficient (re)allocation and use of resources. In addition, competitive pressure serves as an important incentive for firms to innovate – although fierce competition might discourage incremental innovation (Aghion *et al.*, 2002). Further, competition may facilitate labour adjustment through higher firm turnover. The OECD Product Market Regulation (PMR) indicator suggests that, despite recent progress, scope remains to reduce regulatory barriers to competition in the Netherlands. Moreover, the relatively weak productivity growth performance in key ICT-using services sectors – distribution and finance – appears to be partly attributable to regulatory barriers that limit competition and prevent universally available technologies from being as profitable as in other countries notably the United States, Norway and Sweden.

The Netherlands is making considerable progress in fostering competition. The Dutch Competition Authority (NMa) was made formally independent on 1 July 2005. Furthermore, the government has put a Bill to Parliament giving the NMa greater sanctioning powers – including the authority to fine individuals. In addition, the government plans to enhance the NMa's investigative powers by giving it the authority to search private homes. These initiatives still have to be discussed in Parliament. Corporate governance has been improved significantly – *e.g.*, in the structural regime, co-optation and certification have been abolished.[1] In 2006 a Consumer Authority will be set up to deal with consumer complaints. However, with respect to product market regulation, the Netherlands ranks as a "middle-of-the-road" country – neither being very restrictive nor liberal. The most important areas for further reform are barriers to entrepreneurship and, to a lesser extent, state control. More specifically, the Netherlands has a very unfavourable performance on licence and permit procedures – these procedures being relatively complex, timely and expensive. There are also competitive neutrality problems in the Netherlands that should be dealt with.

Lower productivity growth in the distribution sector explains almost half of the economy-wide shortfall in productivity growth *vis-à-vis* the US, where productivity growth was spurred by new, more productive, "big box" establishments that took full advantage of the benefits of ICT. In the Netherlands, entry in retail and especially the creation of "big box" stores has been restricted. In the financial sector, less integration of markets across the European Union than across the United States partly explains lower productivity growth.

Easing product market regulation

The OECD PMR indicators were developed in the late 1990s to benchmark regulation policies across OECD countries (Nicoletti *et al.*, 1999). The indicators – which have been updated to 2003 (Conway *et al.*, 2005) – summarise a large set of formal rules and regulations that have a bearing on competition in OECD countries. A more detailed description can be found in Annex 4.A1.

In 1998 the Netherlands ranked among the "middle of the road" countries – neither being very restrictive nor liberal. Since then, product market regulation has become more conducive to competition. However, as other OECD countries also made progress, the Netherlands still had an average position in 2003 (Figure 4.1). The overall PMR indicator can be broken down into three sub domains: state control, barriers to entrepreneurship and barriers to trade and investment. Across OECD countries, slightly more progress has been made in reducing state control and barriers to trade and investment than in reducing

Figure 4.1. **Product market regulation**[1]

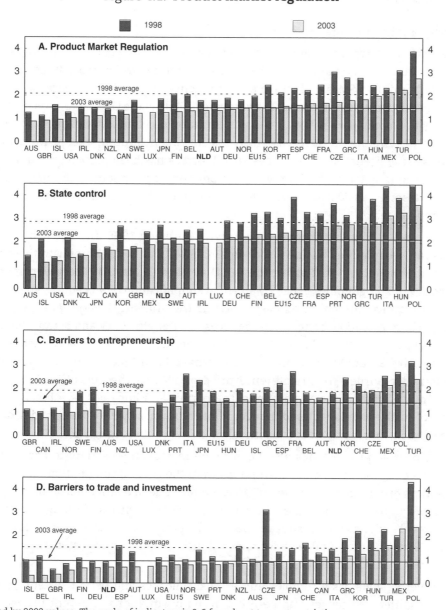

1. Sorted by 2003 values. The scale of indicators is 0-6 from least to most restrictive.

Source: Conway, P., V. Janod, and G. Nicoletti (2005), "Product Market Regulation in OECD Countries, 1998 to 2003", OECD Economics Department Working Paper, No. 419.

barriers to entrepreneurship. Developments in the Netherlands have been more or less similar:

- In 1998, the Netherlands already ranked as a relatively liberal country on barriers to trade and investment and it has since then reduced these barriers further. However, as other OECD countries have removed these barriers more decisively, it is closer to the OECD average in 2003.

- Barriers to entrepreneurship provide the most opportunities for further reform in the Netherlands. In this sub domain, it was a relatively restrictive country in 1998 and – although progress has been made – remains so in 2003.

- To a lesser extent there is also room for improvement in state control. The Netherlands still ranks as a "middle-of-the-road" country, just below the OECD average.

Reducing barriers to entrepreneurship

Barriers to entrepreneurship include regulations and procedures that impose costs and restrictions on companies, *e.g.*, licences and administrative procedures. These are especially harmful to SMEs and pose a barrier to entry for small firms -because they tend to constitute a larger burden for smaller companies. Across the OECD, progress in reducing regulatory and administrative opacity – simplification of administrative procedures – and reduction of burdens on business start-ups has been limited, except for a marked improvement in licence and permit systems. Progress has been particularly limited with respect to removing remaining barriers to competition – exemptions from competition law remain widespread as do legal barriers to new entry in product markets that are sheltered from competition.

In the Netherlands, progress was made between 1998 and 2003 in reducing administrative burdens on business start-ups (Table 4.1), although administrative burdens for corporations remain just above the OECD average (Table 4.2). The government has initiated several programmes explicitly aimed at simplification of procedures and reducing the administrative burden. The *Andere Overheid* (A Different Government) programme focuses on less regulation, better public services, greater efficiency and better cooperation with private organisations. In addition, within the *Administratieve Lasten* (Reduction of Administrative Burden) programme decisions have been taken to reduce the existing administrative burden for private enterprise by 25% by the end of 2007. To reduce administrative burdens for corporations, the permit *Verklaring van geen bezwaar* by the Ministry of Justice that is required to incorporate a business will be abolished. Under the new regulation, incorporation of a business will merely entail registration.

Considerable progress has also been made in reducing barriers to competition – mainly reflecting the abolition of exemptions from the general competition law. However, legal barriers to entry remain above the OECD average due to restrictions on the number of competitors in network industries. Unlike other OECD countries, no progress has been made in regulatory and administrative opacity. The particularly low score on this indicator mainly reflects an unfavourable performance on licence and permit systems – in which no progress was made up until 2003.

The Netherlands has a complex and extensive licence and permit system – totalling almost 900 different licences and permits. In many situations, different licenses from different institutions (*e.g.*, different levels of government) are required for one activity. Costs range from € 3 500 to € 80 000 and statutory response periods are not always

Table 4.1. **Barriers to entrepreneurship**

	Administrative burdens on start-ups		Regulatory and administrative opacity		Barriers to competition	
	1998	2003	1998	2003	1998	2003
Australia	1.1	1.0	1.5	1.2	1.8	1.5
Austria	2.6	2.8	0.6	0.4	1.0	0.8
Belgium	1.3	1.7	3.3	2.2	1.0	0.6
Canada	1.4	0.9	0.6	0.5	0.7	0.7
Czech Republic	2.2	2.3	2.7	2.3	0.6	0.5
Denmark	0.5	0.5	2.4	2.1	2.1	1.7
Finland	2.0	1.3	3.2	1.2	0.7	0.4
France	3.4	1.9	2.7	1.3	1.5	1.4
Germany	2.4	1.6	2.6	2.2	0.4	0.5
Greece	3.0	2.6	1.7	0.6	0.6	0.5
Hungary	2.4	2.3	0.4	0.4	1.5	1.1
Iceland	1.7	1.4	2.7	2.4	0.8	0.7
Ireland	0.9	0.5	2.2	2.1	0.2	0.3
Italy	4.6	2.4	0.7	0.4	1.0	0.6
Japan	2.1	1.9	3.8	1.2	1.0	0.6
Korea	2.2	2.2	3.8	1.2	1.3	1.0
Luxembourg		1.8		1.1		0.1
Mexico	3.4	3.1	2.4	0.4	1.4	2.9
Netherlands	**1.8**	**1.6**	**2.4**	**2.5**	**1.2**	**0.6**
New Zealand	1.0	0.8	2.2	2.2	0.4	0.4
Norway	1.8	1.0	1.3	1.2	0.8	0.6
Poland	3.8	3.7	2.0	1.5	1.6	0.3
Portugal	2.1	1.7	1.8	1.2	1.0	0.5
Slovak Republic		1.9		0.7		0.3
Spain	3.5	2.8	1.6	0.4	0.5	0.4
Sweden	1.1	1.2	3.5	1.1	1.3	0.6
Switzerland	2.2	1.7	3.4	3.1	0.8	0.7
Turkey	2.7	2.7	4.1	3.4	3.2	0.5
United Kingdom	1.0	0.7	1.7	1.2	0.7	0.4
United States	0.9	1.0	2.3	1.3	1.5	1.5
Average	2.0	1.8	2.1	1.4	1.0	0.8

Note: The scale of indicators is 0-6 from least to most restrictive.

Source: Conway, P., Janod, V. and Nicoletti, G. (2005), "Product Market Regulation in OECD Countries, 1998 to 2003", OECD Economics Department Working Paper, No. 419.

respected (Sitra consulting, 2005). PricewaterhouseCoopers (2005) compared the Dutch licence and permit system with that in Denmark, Nordrhein Westfalen (Germany), the UK, Ireland and Spain. It found that the number of licences required to set-up a company is comparable but that the costs are higher and the response time is longer in the Netherlands.

In 2004, the government installed a Taskforce Vereenvoudiging Vergunningen (Simplification of licence and permit procedures) which published its advice in June 2005. A Programme "Simplification of licence and permit procedures" will be set-up to implement most of the Taskforce's recommendations. Among other things, it will review all licences to see whether they are necessary, investigate for which licences a silencio positive (silence is consent) rule can be implemented,[2] try to come to an agreement about the implementation of "shared services" with provinces and municipalities, and start pilots to simplify procedures in situations where more than one licence is required for one activity. A number of OECD countries already use a "silence is consent" rule (i.e., that

Table 4.2. **Selected lower level indicators of barriers to entrepreneurship**

	Regulatory and administrative opacity		Administrative burdens on start-ups		Barriers to competition	
	Licence and permits system		Administrative burdens for corporations		Legal barriers	
	1998	2003	1998	2003	1998	2003
Australia	2.0	2.0	1.0	1.3	1.9	1.6
Austria	0.0	0.0	2.8	3.0	3.5	0.3
Belgium	6.0	4.0	1.5	1.8	1.4	1.6
Canada	0.0	0.0	1.5	0.8	0.8	0.9
Czech Republic	4.0	4.0	3.0	3.0	1.6	1.4
Denmark	4.0	4.0	0.5	1.0	2.3	1.4
Finland	4.0	2.0	1.5	1.3	1.6	1.4
France	4.0	2.0	3.3	2.0	2.0	2.2
Germany	4.0	4.0	2.3	2.3	1.1	1.4
Greece	2.0	0.0	3.0	2.3	1.6	1.6
Hungary	0.0	0.0	2.3	2.3	2.7	1.6
Iceland	4.0	4.0	1.3	1.3	2.3	2.3
Ireland	4.0	4.0	1.5	0.8	0.6	0.9
Italy	0.0	0.0	5.5	2.8	3.3	1.9
Japan	6.0	2.0	2.3	1.5	2.2	1.4
Korea	6.0	2.0	2.7	2.7	2.5	1.9
Luxembourg	0.2	2.0	0.8	2.5		0.3
Mexico	4.0	0.0	3.3	3.3	2.2	1.9
Netherlands	**4.0**	**4.0**	**2.0**	**2.0**	**2.2**	**1.9**
New Zealand	4.0	4.0	1.0	1.0	0.3	0.3
Norway	2.0	2.0	1.9	1.0	2.7	2.2
Poland	2.0	2.0	4.3	4.3	1.6	0.6
Portugal	2.0	0.0	2.8	1.5	1.2	1.4
Slovak Republic		0.0		2.0		0.6
Spain	2.0	0.0	3.5	2.8	1.4	1.1
Sweden	6.0	2.0	1.3	1.0	2.0	2.0
Switzerland	6.0	6.0	3.3	2.3	2.5	2.2
Turkey	6.0	6.0	2.3	2.3	2.2	1.4
United Kingdom	3.0	2.0	0.8	0.8	1.4	1.4
United States	4.0	2.0	0.5	0.8	1.1	1.4
Average	3.2	2.2	2.1	1.9	1.7	1.4

Note: The scale of indicators is 0-6 from least to most restrictive.

Source: Conway, P., Janod, V. and Nicoletti, G. (2005), "Product Market Regulation in OECD Countries, 1998 to 2003", *OECD Economics Department Working Paper*, No. 419.

licenses are issued automatically if the licensing office has not acted by the end of the statutory response period). This increases incentives to respect the statutory response period and might reduce response time in the Netherlands. The implementation of "shared services" could be a first step to introduce single contact points ("one-stop shops") for issuing licenses. Given the different institutions involved, the creation of single contact points can result in a large reduction in costs, administrative burden and complexity for companies.

Preventing distortions to competition from state control

The reduction in state control in the OECD has, in large part, been due to the easing or elimination of involvement in business operation – command-and-control measures and price controls. In contrast, on average, there has not been a great deal of privatisation undertaken – as reflected in the indicator of public ownership. The same holds for the

Netherlands, where involvement in business operation was already low in 1998 and has been reduced further (Table 4.3). Its ranking on public ownership is average – reflecting the degree of state ownership of enterprises (size and scope of the public sector) and the incidence of "golden shares" (direct control over business enterprises) (Table 4.4).

Table 4.3. **Indicators of state control**

	Public ownership		Involvement in business operation	
	1998	2003	1998	2003
Australia	1.1	0.8	1.9	0.3
Austria	2.7	2.2	2.3	1.6
Belgium	2.8	2.2	4.0	2.6
Canada	1.8	1.7	1.8	1.5
Czech Republic	4.8	3.0	2.9	1.9
Denmark	2.2	1.7	2.1	0.8
Finland	3.7	3.2	2.6	1.3
France	3.5	3.3	3.0	1.9
Germany	3.0	2.8	2.9	1.5
Greece	4.2	2.4	4.9	3.3
Hungary	4.5	3.8	3.3	2.6
Iceland	2.4	1.8	1.8	0.3
Ireland	2.5	1.8	2.7	2.1
Italy	5.1	3.8	3.6	2.3
Japan	0.9	0.8	3.3	2.4
Korea	3.0	1.8	2.2	1.5
Luxembourg	–	2.6	–	1.2
Mexico	2.5	2.3	2.3	1.4
Netherlands	**3.3**	**2.5**	**2.0**	**1.2**
New Zealand	1.5	1.9	1.4	0.8
Norway	3.7	3.5	2.5	1.8
Poland	5.3	4.2	3.6	2.8
Portugal	3.6	3.1	3.8	2.2
Slovak Republic		1.9		0.8
Spain	3.0	2.7	3.5	2.7
Sweden	2.7	2.2	1.5	1.6
Switzerland	2.7	2.4	3.0	2.1
Turkey	3.7	3.1	4.1	2.5
United Kingdom	1.8	1.9	1.8	1.6
Kingdom States	1.3	1.2	1.4	1.2
Average	3.0	2.4	2.7	1.7

Note: The scale of indicators is 0-6 from least to most restrictive.

Source: Conway, P., Janod, V. and Nicoletti, G. (2005), "Product Market Regulation in OECD Countries, 1998 to 2003", OECD Economics Department Working Paper, No. 419.

State ownership is mainly concentrated in the network sectors like energy (gas and electricity), post and telecommunications and transport (rail, bus and air). Earlier OECD work has found cross-country evidence that liberalisation policies in network industries have led to higher productivity, better quality and, often, lower prices (OECD, 2001). The government has different objectives which may conflict with the aim of promoting competition. Privatisation plays an important role in eliminating possible conflicts of interest. In spite of this, the pace of structural reform and privatisation of network sectors has slowed in the Netherlands; for instance, the privatisation of Schiphol airport has been discussed since 1995 and Parliament only recently agreed to sell a minority of government

Table 4.4. **Lower level indicators of state control**

Public ownership

	Scope of public enterprise sector		Size of public enterprise sector		Direct control over business enterprise	
	1998	2003	1998	2003	1998	2003
Australia	2.8	2.8	0.8	0.1	0.0	0.0
Austria	5.0	3.5	4.3	4.0	0.0	0.0
Belgium	2.3	1.8	3.3	3.3	2.6	1.5
Canada	2.8	2.8	2.1	2.1	0.8	0.8
Czech Republic	4.5	3.8	4.5	3.2	5.3	2.3
Denmark	3.0	2.5	2.3	2.3	1.5	0.8
Finland	3.5	3.5	4.2	3.2	3.6	2.9
France	5.0	4.5	4.3	4.1	1.9	1.9
Germany	3.5	3.3	3.4	3.2	2.3	2.3
Greece	3.3	3.0	4.4	3.8	4.6	0.9
Hungary	4.5	3.5	3.4	3.0	5.3	4.8
Iceland	2.8	2.3	3.3	2.8	1.4	0.7
Ireland	3.0	2.5	3.3	2.6	1.5	0.8
Italy	5.3	4.5	4.2	3.7	5.6	3.5
Japan	2.0	2.0	0.0	0.0	0.6	0.6
Korea	2.3	2.0	3.4	2.8	3.4	1.0
Luxembourg	1.9	3.5	1.2	1.2	1.3	2.9
Mexico	3.5	3.0	3.7	3.6	1.1	0.9
Netherlands	**3.0**	**2.8**	**3.2**	**2.8**	**3.8**	**2.0**
New Zealand	1.5	2.3	1.0	0.8	2.0	2.6
Norway	4.8	4.8	4.6	4.0	2.4	2.4
Poland	6.0	5.8	5.4	4.6	4.9	3.0
Portugal	3.9	3.8	2.5	1.7	4.2	3.8
Slovak Republic		1.6		0.0		3.5
Spain	4.5	3.5	2.7	2.5	2.3	2.3
Sweden	3.7	3.7	3.2	2.7	1.8	0.7
Switzerland	3.8	3.8	0.9	0.9	3.4	2.6
Turkey	4.8	4.8	4.5	4.3	2.4	1.0
United States	0.8	0.8	1.7	1.6	2.6	2.9
United Kingdom	2.8	2.5	0.6	0.6	0.8	0.8
Average	3.4	3.1	3.0	2.5	2.5	1.9

Note: The scale of indicators is 0-6 from least to most restrictive.

Source: Conway, P., Janod, V. and Nicoletti, G. (2005), "Product Market Regulation in OECD Countries, 1998 to 2003", OECD Economics Department Working Paper, No. 419.

shares. Local government ownership still persists in public transport and electricity and gas distribution networks. This can act as a barrier to access the network for third parties and makes the regulator's task more difficult.

The Dutch government also retains golden shares in the incumbent telecoms and postal operators. Although the government has minority stakes in these companies, the golden shares grant the government special rights e.g., in case of merger with or acquisition by another company. Golden shares, by hindering the market for corporate control, strongly reduce the positive effects of privatisation and are a strong disincentive for investment. Without being explicitly discriminatory, these special powers are liable to make it more difficult to acquire shareholdings in the firms concerned and therefore deter investors from other Member States from investing in their capital. For this reason, the European Commission has taken the Netherlands to the European Court of Justice over the golden shares in KPN (telecom) and TNT (post). The government has recently reduced its minority stakes further and has stated that the golden shares will be relinquished when its stake falls below 10%. The Dutch State plans to lose its golden share before the end of 2005, as its stake in Royal KPN is now at 8%.

Besides conflicts of interest, publicly-owned enterprises can distort competition in markets where they compete with private sector enterprises – leading to competitive neutrality problems. These problems can arise when competition is distorted by the advantages that some government businesses have due to their government ownership, *e.g.*, different regulations, lower costs of capital, exemptions from competition law and subsidies to fund public service obligations. Based on a number of case studies – including local public transport and commercial activities of institutions for vocational education – PricewaterhouseCoopers (2005) recently concluded that competitive neutrality problems persist in the Netherlands. Although internationally comparable data on the total economic costs of these distortions are not readily available, countries that have limited the number of public sector businesses that provide goods or services in competition with the private sector or have enshrined competitive neutrality principles in policies on corporate governance or competition law (such as in New Zealand) are known to have significantly reduced neutrality problems (OECD, 2005).

The European Community, Australia, Finland and Sweden have all placed a priority on dealing directly with competitive neutrality problems. In the Netherlands, the relationship between the public and the private sector has been a topic of debate since 1995. The Dutch government plans to put a Market and Government Bill to Parliament in the spring of 2006. It is intended that this Bill will incorporate rules of conduct for public bodies in the Dutch Competition Act. Four rules are being considered: *i)* a ban on cross-subsidies; *ii)* a ban on the exclusive use of data that the organisation has gathered in order to exercise its public mandate; *iii)* a ban on the intermingling of public and commercial responsibilities; and *iv)* a ban on preferential treatment for public enterprises. The potential advantages of explicit competitive neutrality frameworks are large. However, considerable commitment, and often cultural change, is needed among public sector businesses, the agencies responsible for those businesses, policy agencies and politicians at all levels of government (national, regional and local).

Without commitment to uphold the rules, benefits will not be realised. The recent discussion on the Dutch rental raising market provides an example with respect to the intermingling of public and commercial responsibilities. A large share of the rental market in the Netherlands consists of (subsidised) social housing, which is the responsibility of social housing corporations (private organisations with public activities).[3] Part of this social housing is rented to high income households. This is distorting the private rental market and the European Commission declared that such arrangements constitute unfair competition under the European competition law. Consequently, the Commission required that Dutch social housing corporations sell part of their housing stock in case of structural and excessive overcapacity. This has led to a number of protests both within and outside the government. An alternative might be to restrict access to subsidised rentals to low-income households and charge market rates for other tenants. The government is preparing a strategy document setting out its vision on social housing corporations that should be finished in 2005. Creating a level playing field in the rental market and dealing with the remarks of the Commission on state aid are main parts of this vision.

Fostering productivity growth in services

Retail trade

Lower productivity growth in the distribution sector – consisting of retail and wholesale trade – explains almost half of the economy-wide shortfall in productivity growth vis-à-vis the US in recent years (Chapter 1). The productivity growth differential between the US and the EU is sometimes attributed to incomparable data and inadequate measurement methods. However, recent research by the GGDC (Groningen Growth and Development Centre) tried to harmonise data and found the growth differential in retail is real (Timmer and Inklaar, 2005).[4] In the US, productivity growth was spurred by more productive entering establishments displacing much less productive exiting establishments (Foster et al., 2002). These new, more productive stores tended to be "big box" establishments that took full advantage of the benefits of ICT; for instance, linking barcodes to ICT (Electronic Data Interchange) has resulted in more efficient use of shelf space, trucking and shipping, and reduced inventory (Conference Board, 2005). In spite of fast productivity growth, employment has not declined, but instead it has been growing relatively strongly in the retail and wholesale sector in the US (Figure 4.2).

Figure 4.2. **Employment growth in retail for selected countries**

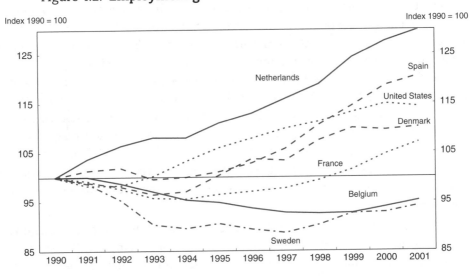

Source: OECD STAN database.

Using the PMR database, indicators of regulation in retail distribution have been constructed. The summary indicator suggests that the Netherlands has one of the least restrictive environments for retail (Figure 4.3). Its position on "price controls" and "barriers to entry" (abstracting from zoning regulations – see below) is particularly favourable – the latter mainly reflecting that no specific licence or notification to authorities is needed for selling food or clothing. The somewhat less favourable score on "business restrictions" mainly reflects a less liberalised stance on shop opening hours than in other OECD countries. Although maximum shop opening hours were increased from 55 to 96 per week in 1996, shops are not allowed to open on Sundays unless they are exempt from the general regulation (as, for example, are shops in tourist areas). This compares less favourably to countries where no restrictions exist, e.g., the US and Sweden. Overall, it would seem that productivity growth in retail has not been hampered very much by product market regulations.

Figure 4.3. **Indicators of regulation in retail distribution**[1]

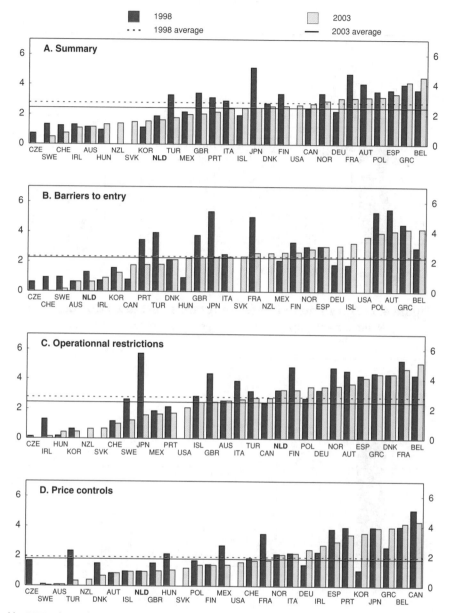

1. Sorted by 2003 values. The scale of indicators is 0-6 from least to most restrictive.
Source: Conway, P. and Nicoletti, G. (2006), "The OECD Indicators of Product Market Regulation", *OECD Economics Department Working Papers*, forthcoming.

However, indirect indicators of the intensity of product market competition seem to present a less favourable picture. Mark-ups in retail and wholesale are relatively high (Figure 4.4). Although data on foreign affiliates and entry and exit is relatively limited, it seems to point in the same direction. Compared to other European countries, entry and exit rates in the Dutch retail sector are relatively low (Figure 4.5). Especially in a small country like the Netherlands, foreign affiliates can make an important contribution to increased competition. Value-added of foreign affiliates in relation to total value-added in the retail, wholesale and hotel sector seems to have been rising until 1999, but has since fallen back to only slightly above the 1996 level (Figure 4.6). The indicators could suggest that entry barriers are relatively high in the Netherlands, limiting competition.

Figure 4.4. **Mark-ups in retail and wholesale in selected OECD countries**

Average mark-ups 1975-2002

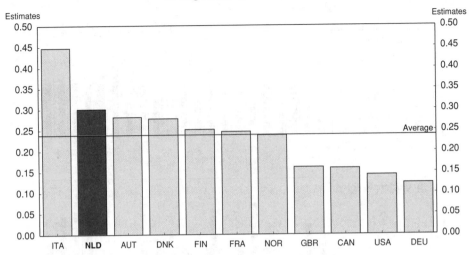

Source: OECD STAN database.

Figure 4.5. **Entry and exit rates in retail, selected OECD countries**

Number of entering/exiting firms as percentage of total, 1998-2000

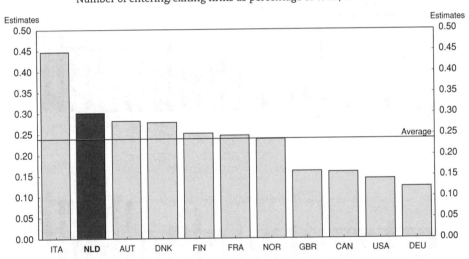

Source: Eurostat.

The seeming contradiction between indicators of regulation and indicators of the intensity of competition might be due to strict planning and zoning regulations that are not fully reflected in the indicators of regulation in retail distribution. Zoning regulations increase the costs of building new stores and artificially inflate the value of old stores based on the land they occupy – making exit less likely. This might limit entry and, thereby, competition. In the Netherlands, land use policies are relevant for all store sizes – as opposed to France (above 300 m^2) and Germany (1 200 m^2) (The Conference Board, 2005) – and are mainly the responsibility of municipalities. The relatively low intensity of competition – as suggested by the high mark-ups, and below average entry and exit rates and – might indicate that land use policies of municipalities have been strict. Indeed, municipalities might have an incentive to favour local insiders.

OECD ECONOMIC SURVEYS: NETHERLANDS – ISBN 92-64-03669-5 – © OECD 2006

Figure 4.4. **Mark-ups in retail and wholesale in selected OECD countries**

Average mark-ups 1975-2002

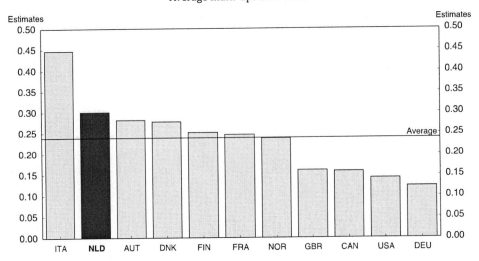

Source: OECD STAN database.

Figure 4.5. **Entry and exit rates in retail, selected OECD countries**

Number of entering/exiting firms as percentage of total, 1998-2000

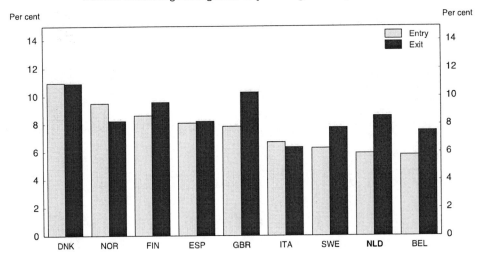

Source: Eurostat.

The seeming contradiction between indicators of regulation and indicators of the intensity of competition might be due to strict planning and zoning regulations that are not fully reflected in the indicators of regulation in retail distribution. Zoning regulations increase the costs of building new stores and artificially inflate the value of old stores based on the land they occupy – making exit less likely. This might limit entry and, thereby, competition. In the Netherlands, land use policies are relevant for all store sizes – as opposed to France (above 300 m²) and Germany (1 200 m²) (The Conference Board, 2005) – and are mainly the responsibility of municipalities. The relatively low intensity of competition – as suggested by the high mark-ups, and below average entry and exit rates and – might indicate that land use policies of municipalities have been strict. Indeed, municipalities might have an incentive to favour local insiders.

Figure 4.6. **Growth of foreign affiliates in retail and wholesale, selected OECD countries**

Value added by foreign firms/total value added, 1996 = 100

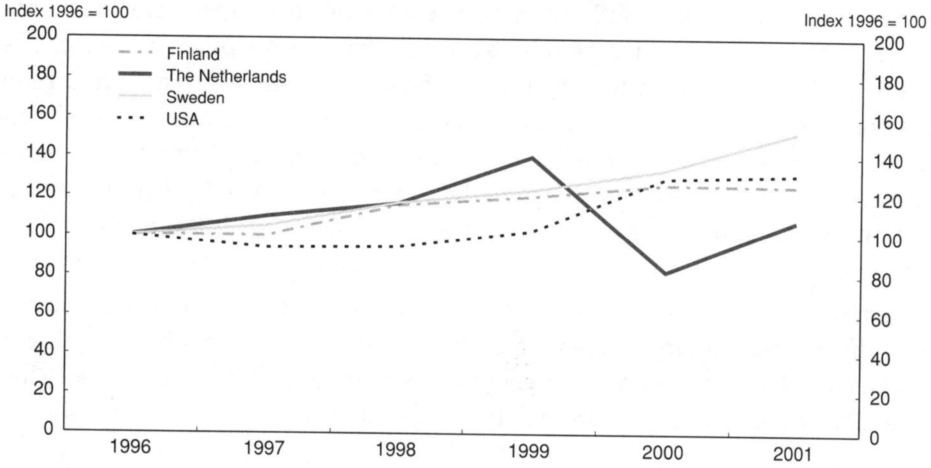

Source: OECD AFA, FATS and STAN databases 2004.

In addition, barriers to the development of "big box" stores might have reduced competition and productivity growth. Until recently, the Dutch central government had detailed rules for the establishment of large shopping centres or mega stores on the edge of towns through the PDV/GDV policy (*i.e.,* policy on peripheral and large-scale retail outlets). The establishment of retail outlets on city fringes, or of very large shopping centres, was severely prescribed by these restrictions with the objective of protecting shopping in town centres. These regulations have prevented the development of "big box" stores in most merchandise – notably food and general merchandise – that have been established in other countries. In contrast, large furniture and building materials stores have been allowed to open. The Dutch authorities consider that this policy has contributed to maintaining a large number and diversity of stores in inner cities (including in historical city centres), which is valued by the Dutch population. Although the optimal structure for retail distribution might ultimately be somewhat different for Europe than for the US – due to for example cultural differences – larger retail outlets, providing one-stop shop services, offer greater convenience and lower prices arising from improved efficiency and resulting in cost savings that are passed on to consumers. Moreover, evidence seems to suggest that fears of a decline in traditional retailing offering specialisation or location convenience are exaggerated and that small shops can survive because consumers are willing to pay a premium for their services (Dobson and Waterson, 1999). Thus, it seems that the process that spurred productivity growth in the US – through the profitable use of ICT and economies of scale – has been hindered in the Netherlands.

Recently, the PDV/GDV policy has been abolished and the decision-making power on the location of large retail outlets has been largely decentralised to provinces and municipalities. However, a restriction has been imposed: the establishment of large, peripheral retail outlets should not have a negative impact on the existing retail trade structure (*verzorgingsstructuur*) in inner cities and shopping centres. To monitor this, the provincial governments have to draw up zoning plans for retail and wholesale trade, which have to be approved by the central government. This restriction might turn out to be as restrictive as the PDV/GDV policy, hindering the entry of new large stores. In addition, decentralising decision making power to local government is not without risk for competition. Experience from other countries (e.g., Italy and the United Kingdom) suggests that entry by large format stores may become more difficult as local authorities may be more inclined to protect incumbents and thus less likely to grant planning permission. Local governments might be less inclined to protect incumbent interests if they had higher financial incentives to attract large out of town stores. For instance, the government could consider letting the local governments share to a larger extent in the benefits of attracting new large retail stores, e.g., through a share in retail trade related taxes. Altogether, competition would be enhanced if the restriction regarding retail trade structure were abolished and if the decisions of local governments were overseen to ensure that they do not unduly favour incumbent interests

In addition, regulations on store opening hours reduce economies of scale[5] and, thereby, the creation of large stores. Thus, further liberalisation of shop opening hours should be considered to enhance the possibilities to reap the benefits of scale. The 1996 liberalisation of shop opening hours is to be evaluated in 2006.

Financial services

Financial services account for the rest of the gap in productivity growth vis-à-vis the US. Traditional indicators of the degree of competition – e.g., prices, costs and margins – suggest that the intensity of market forces in the Netherlands is relatively high. However, this may also be the result of economies of scale. The concentration in the Dutch banking sector is relatively high – with three firms representing 75% of total assets. High switching costs (MEA, 2002) and a lack of transparency (AFM, 2004) are seen as important obstacles in the retail financial market.

Lower productivity growth in Dutch financial services is partly attributable to the fact that markets are less integrated across the European Union than they are across the United States. However, progress is being made towards financial market integration in Europe. This is most evident in wholesale financial markets (EC, 2004). Where integration has occurred, it has been stimulated by market forces leading to the establishment of common pan-European infrastructures. The search for consolidation-based efficiency gains, the early stages of the implementation of the Financial Services Action Plan (FSAP) (ibid.)[6], and the creation of the euro seem to have accelerated these changes (ECB, 2004).

Little integration has occurred, however, in retail banking services – i.e., services for consumers and SMEs (EC, 2004). Greater integration of these services will occur to some extent through market developments, notably consolidation of trading and settlement infrastructure. However, policy actions will also be required, in particular implementation of the FSAP and the extended application of the four level "Lamfalussy framework"[7]. With respect to retail markets the EC has identified six key areas for action: information and transparency, redress procedures, balanced application of consumer protection rules, electronic commerce, insurance intermediaries and cross-border retail payments.[8]

It will be important that the Netherlands, as other European governments, does not stand in the way of retail banking consolidation across national borders in the name of defending national champions. In addition, the Netherlands should reduce remaining barriers in the financial retail market to improve its productivity performance; the EC for instance, identifies the portability of bank accounts as an area of possible future action to reduce obstacles to opening an account across borders. The Netherlands should introduce domestic portability of bank accounts in anticipation of market integration and to improve domestic performance. In addition, simplified products in financial retail services can both contribute to more transparency and a greater comparability between products in different European countries. A report for the EC identified that there is a large scope for simplification of products (Charles River Associates, 2004).

Conclusion

Like the US, the Netherlands has a high level of productivity. However, productivity growth has been one of the weakest of the OECD in recent years and the economy therefore risks losing its edge. This has been partly due to product market regulations, where, although progress has been made, the Netherlands still ranks as a "middle-of-the-road" country. Opportunities for improvement are mainly in the domains of barriers to entrepreneurship and state control: more specifically, improving licence and permit procedures and preventing competitive neutrality problems. Productivity growth has been especially unfavourable in the ICT-using services – distribution and finance. In retail trade, this is partly due to restrictions on entry, especially of large stores. In the financial services this is partly due to less integrated markets across the European Union than across the United States. However, reducing domestic barriers to competition – e.g., non-portability of bank accounts – might improve performance and anticipate a more integrated market. Detailed recommendations are provided in Box 4.1.

Box 4.1. **Policy recommendations to ease the strictness of product market regulations**

Reform of product market regulation

The government should reduce product market regulation, notably in the domains of barriers to entrepreneurship and state control:

- To reduce barriers to entrepreneurship, the government should:
  - ❖ implement a "silence is consent" rule for issuing licenses in cases where there are no severe (dangerous) consequences for society, the rights and duties of companies are clear and third party interests are not harmed; and
  - ❖ introduce single contact points ("one-stop shops") for issuing licenses.
- To reduce (the adverse effects of) state control, the government should:
  - ❖ relinquish golden shares in the incumbent telecoms and postal operators; and
  - ❖ introduce rules of conduct for public bodies to prevent competitive neutrality problems.

Retail and financial sectors

The government should foster productivity growth in the retail and financial sectors, through reducing regulatory barriers:

- To increase competition in retail trade, the government should:
  - ❖ abolish restrictions on the development of large stores;
  - ❖ monitor local governments to ensure that they are not unduly responsive to incumbent interests;
  - ❖ consider increasing the financial incentive for municipalities to attract large out-of-town stores, e.g., through a share in retail trade related taxes; and
  - ❖ consider further liberalisation of shop opening hours;
- To improve performance of financial services, the government should:
  - ❖ foster the European integration of retail financial markets; and
  - ❖ introduce portability of bank accounts.

Notes

1. Co-optation: existing members of the supervisory board select the new members. Certification: the trust office holds shares and in their place issues non-voting certificates, with the corresponding shares' voting rights generally being available to the Board.

2. A "silence is consent" rule will only be implemented in the Netherlands if: there are no severe (dangerous) consequences for society; the rights and duties of companies are clear; and third party interests are not harmed.

3. The government transferred € 16.7 billion to social housing corporations in 1995, representing the present value of future subsidies to which they were entitled.

4. The GGDC 60-Industry Database is based on the OECD STAN Database. However, in order to reach a greater degree of industry detail, and to provide a comprehensive dataset without gaps, OECD STAN data were complemented with information from industry and services statistics and additional (historical) national accounts data for individual countries.

5. The Conference Board (2005) identifies three channels through which store hour restrictions can reduce the incentive to build large stores:

   ● Decreased shopping: without long opening hours, some items are simply not purchased by consumers because they do not have the time to sift through all these choices if hours are constrained.

   ● Reduced convenience: consumers are willing to trade-off longer travel times for the convenience of one-stop shopping. However, that trip is not possible if the store is not open when the consumer can go.

   ● Less scheduling flexibility: if closing hours are early, the consumer will not see it as possible to reap the advantages of the large format store, as the risk of "arriving late" is too high to justify the extra trip.

6. The Financial Services Action Plan is a regulatory reform programme aimed at removing barriers to the integration of financial markets across the EU. Future priorities, in addition to implementing successfully what has already been agreed, include the rapid adoption by Parliament and Council of the 8th Company Law Directive on Statutory Audit and of forthcoming European Commission proposals for a third Money Laundering Directive and for a Directive on Capital Adequacy (European Commission Press Release IP/04/696, 1 June 2004).

7. The Lamfalussy framework only applies to securities market regulation for the time being. The four levels of the framework are as follows:

   ● The EC, in consultation with the European Parliament and European Council, reaches agreement on framework principles and the definition of implementing powers in the proposed Directive/Regulation.

   ● The EC, after consulting with the European Securities Committee, requests advice from the European Securities Regulators Committee on technical implementing measures. This culminates in a proposal that is adopted by the EC if approved by the European Securities Committee.

   ● The European Securities Regulators Committee works on joint interpretation recommendations, consistent guidelines and common standards (in areas not covered by EU legislation), peer review, and compares regulatory practice to ensure consistent implementation and application.

   ● The EC checks Member State compliance with EU legislation and may take legal action against any member State suspected of breaching Community Law.

8. http://europa.eu.int/scadplus/leg/en/lvb/l24210.htm.

Bibliography

AFM (2004), *evaluatie van de bijsluiter* (evaluation of the information notice), Dutch only.

Aghion, P., Bloom, N., Blundell, R., Gri¢th, R. and Howitt, P. (2002), *Competition and Innovation: An Inverted U Relationship*, The Institute for Fiscal Studies, WP02/04.

Charles River Associates (2004), *An assessment of the extent of an identified need for simplified, standard financial services products*.

Conference Board (2005), *The Retail Revolution: Can Europe Match US Productivity Performance?*, Perspectives on a global economy, research report R-1358-05-RR.

Conway, P., Janod, V. and Nicoletti, G. (2005), "Product Market Regulation in OECD Countries, 1998 to 2003", *OECD Economics Department Working Paper*, No. 419.

Conway, P. and Nicoletti, G. (2006), "The OECD Indicators of Product Market Regulation", *OECD Economics Department Working Papers,* forthcoming.

Dobson, P. and Waterson, M. (1999), *Retail Power: Recent Developments and Policy Implications, Economic Policy*, No. 28, p. 135-164.

European Central Bank (ECB) (2004), *Measuring Financial Integration in the Euro Area, Occasional Paper,* No. 14, April.

European Commission (EC) (2004), *Financial Integration Monitor,* Commission Staff Working Document SEC (2004) 559.

Foster, L. Haltiwanger, J. and Krizan, C.J. (2002), *The Link Between Aggregate and Micro Productivity Growth: Evidence From Retail Trade,* NBER Working Paper Series, Working Paper 9120.

Nicoletti, G., Scarpetta, S. and Boylaud, O. (1999), "Summary Indicators of Product Market Regulation with an Extension to Employment Protection Legislation", *OECD Economics Department Working Papers,* No. 226.

Ministry of Economic Affairs (2002), *Kosten nog moeite, Drempels slechten voor de switchende consument* (Costs nor pains, Lowering barriers for switching consumers), Dutch only.

OECD (2001), *OECD Economic Survey the United States,* OECD, Paris.

OECD (2005), *Regulating Market Activities by Public Sector,* DAF/COMP(2004)26.

PricewaterhouseCoopers (2005), *Onderzoek naar de problematiek Markt en Overheid* (Review of the problems of Market and Government), Dutch only.

Sitra consulting (2005), *Kosten en effecten van vergunningverlening: inventarisatie naar de kenmerken van 77 geselecteerde vergunningstelsels* (Costs and effects of licence procedures), Dutch only.

Taskforce Vereenvoudiging Vergunningen (2005), *Eenvoudig Vergunnen* (Simplyfication of licence procedures), Dutch only.

Timmer, M.P. and Inklaar, R. (2005), *Productivity differentials in the US and EU distributive trade sector: statistical myth or reality?*, Groningen Growth and Development Centre, University of Groningen.

ANNEX 4.A1

The Product Market Regulation indicator system[1]

The structure of the Product Market Regulation indicator system is shown in Figure 4.A1.1. The system is in the form of a pyramid with 16 low-level indicators at the base and one overall indicator of product market regulation at the top. Each of the low-level indicators captures a specific aspect of the regulatory regime. In total, the low-level

Figure 4.A1.1. **The PMR indicator system[1]**

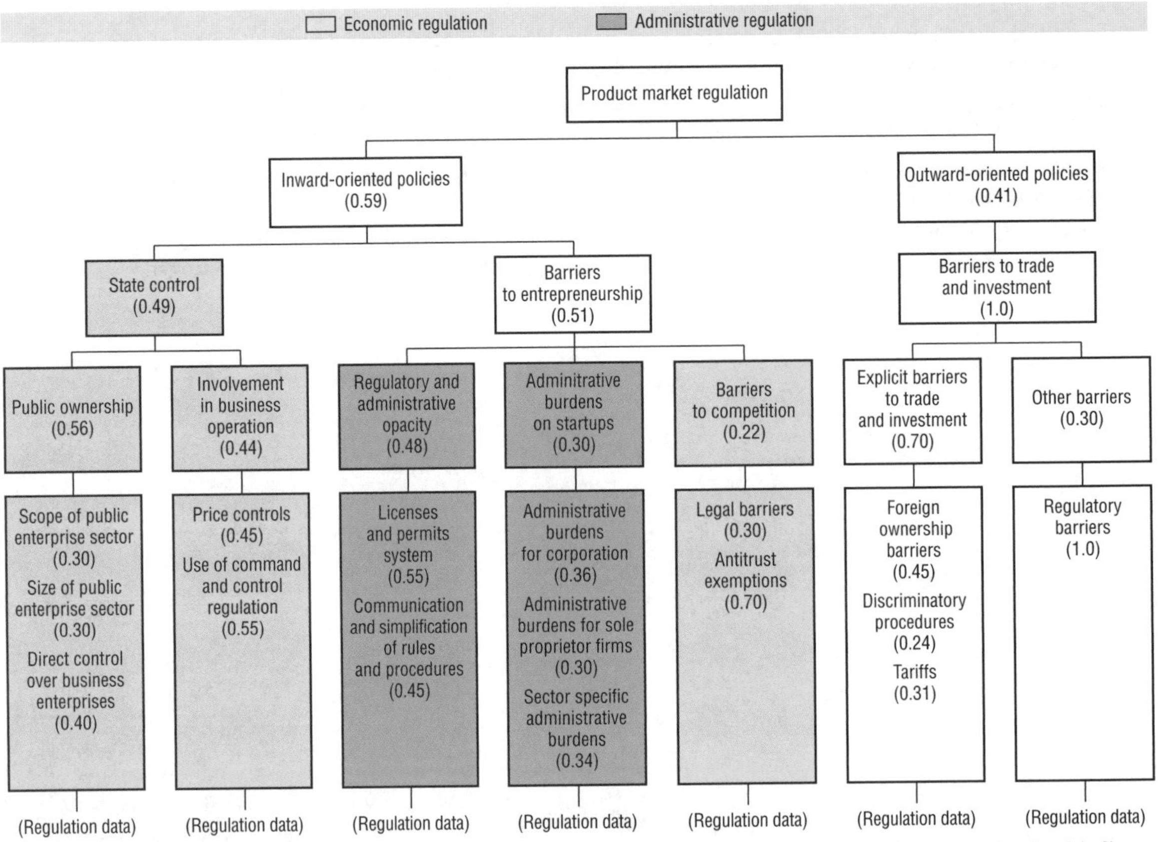

1. The numbers in brackets indicate the weight given to each lower level indicator in the calculation of the higher level indicator immediately above it. The weights were derived by applying principal components analysis to the set of indicators in each of the main regulatory domains (state control, barriers to entrepreneurship, barriers to trade and investment, economic regulation and administrative regulation). The same approach was used to derive the weights used to calculate the indicators of inward and outward-oriented policies and the overall PMR indicator. The principal components analysis was based on the original 1998 data.

Source: Conway, P., V. Janod, and G. Nicoletti (2005), "Product Market Regulation in OECD Countries, 1998 to 2003", *OECD Economics Department Working Paper*, No. 419.

indicators span most of the important aspects of general regulatory practice as well as some aspects of industry-specific regulatory policies (in particular, in retail distribution, air and rail passenger transport, rail and road freight, telecommunications) (Box 4A1.1).

Box 4A1.1. **The low-level PMR indicators**

There are 16 low-level indicators in the PMR system. These indicators cover a wide range of product market policies. This box gives a brief description of each low-level indicator. Comprehensive details on the data and methodology used to construct the low-level indicators are provided in the annex.

Scope of public enterprises: this indicator measures the pervasiveness of state ownership across business sectors as the proportion of sectors in which the state has an equity stake in at least one firm.

Size of public enterprise: reflects the overall size of state-owned enterprises relative to the size of the economy.

Direct control over business enterprises: measures the existence of government special voting rights in privately-owned firms, constraints on the sale of state-owned equity stakes, and the extent to which legislative bodies control the strategic choices of public enterprises.

Price controls: reflects the extent of price controls in specific sectors.

Use of command and control regulation: indicates the extent to which government uses coercive (as opposed to incentive-based) regulation in general and in specific service sectors.

Licenses and permits systems: reflects the use of "one-stop shops' and "silence is consent' rules for getting information on and issuing licenses and permits.

Communication and simplification of rules and procedures: reflects aspects of government's communication strategy and efforts to reduce and simplify the administrative burden of interacting with government.

Administrative burdens for corporations: measures the administrative burdens on the creation of corporations.

Administrative burdens for sole proprietors: measures the administrative burdens on the creation of sole proprietor firms.

Sector-specific administrative burdens: reflects administrative burdens in the road transport and retail distribution sectors.

Legal barriers: measures the scope of explicit legal limitations on the number of competitors allowed in a wide range of business sectors.

Antitrust exemptions: measures the scope of exemptions to competition law for public enterprises.

Ownership barriers: reflects legal restrictions on foreign acquisition of equity in public and private firms and in the telecommunications and airlines sectors.

Tariffs: reflects the (simple) average of most-favoured-nation tariffs.

Discriminatory procedures: reflects the extent of discrimination against foreign firms at the procedural level.

Regulatory barriers: reflects other barriers to international trade (*e.g.* international harmonisation, mutual recognition agreements).

To calculate the indicators, the qualitative information contained in the *OECD International Regulation Database* – such as YES/NO answers – is coded by assigning a numerical value to each of the possible responses to a given question. Quantitative information is subdivided into classes using a system of thresholds. The coded information is normalised over a scale of zero to six, reflecting increasing restrictiveness of regulatory provisions for competition. These data are then aggregated into low-level indicators by assigning subjective weights to the various regulatory provisions. Given the normalisation of the basic data all the low-level indicators also have a scale of zero to six. Details of how each of the low-level indicators is calculated, including the weights used in its construction and the techniques used to handle missing data, are given in the annex.

At each step up the pyramid the regulatory domain summarised by the indicators becomes broader. Higher-level indicators are calculated as weighted averages of their constituent lower-level indicators. The attribution of lower-level indicators to each higher-level indicator, and the weights used in the averaging, are based on principal component analysis. For a given regulatory domain this technique reveals sets of lower-level indicators that are most associated with different underlying (unobserved) principal components. In most cases, these principal components represent sub-domains of regulation that can be given a straightforward economic interpretation. Within each principal component, the lower-level indicators are weighted according to the proportion of the cross-country variance of the component that is explained by them. In this way, indicators that have the largest variation across countries are assigned the largest weights.[2] Figure 4.A1.1 provides a summary of the weights used in aggregation.

At the top of the structure the overall indicator of product market regulation summarises the main features of the regulatory framework in the product market of each country. One important advantage of this system is that the value of higher-level indicators can be traced with an increasing degree of detail to the values of the more disaggregated indicators and, eventually, to specific data points in the regulation database. This allows differences in indicator values across time and countries to be decomposed into specific differences in regulation. This is not possible with indicator systems based on opinion surveys, which can identify perceived areas of policy weakness, but cannot attribute these to specific policy settings.

Notes

1. See for the PMR indicator values and the data that were used to construct them: *www.oecd.org/document/1/0,2340,en_2649_37463_2367297_1_1_1_37463,00.html*.

2. More information on factor analysis in the context of the PMR indicators can be found in Nicoletti *et al.* (1999). One downside of weights estimated using this technique is that they are sensitive to revisions in the basic data. As discussed below, the 1998 data on which the weights were originally based has been revised as part of the current update. However, the weights were not re-estimated, partly because the sensitivity analysis presented later suggests that the main conclusions of the paper are to a large extent robust to the choice of weights used in the construction of the indicators.

ISBN 92-64-03669-5
OECD Economic Surveys: Netherlands
© OECD 2006

Chapter 5

Making better use of knowledge creation in innovation activities

This chapter discusses priorities for strengthening innovation in the Netherlands. The main weaknesses are in business R&D intensity, the share of the population with tertiary education, and in commercially applying new knowledge. About 60% of the shortfall in the business R&D intensity relative to the OECD average is linked to the specialisation of the Dutch economy in R&D extensive sectors. The remaining 40% can be explained by a number of factors, including low R&D intensity of inward FDI. Strengthening co-operation between public research organisations and innovating firms, rationalising support for innovation and increasing both the current and prospective supply of scientists and engineers would help to make the Netherlands a more attractive location for R&D investments. Factors that weigh down tertiary education attainment appear to be, the absence of shorter (2-year) courses especially at a tertiary vocational level, and inadequate incentives for institutions to attract students. The authorities are considering introducing shorter tertiary courses and are experimenting with greater competition among tertiary education suppliers for public funds. Barriers to entrepreneurship contribute to the weak performance in commercially applying new knowledge. The government is encouraging entrepreneurship, notably through education campaigns and reform of bankruptcy laws, but more should be done to strengthen incentives for entrepreneurship.

Introduction

The Netherlands has an excellent record in knowledge *creation* but a mediocre record in innovation activity, which is defined as the successful *development* and *application* of new knowledge in new products and/or processes.[1] Key innovation indicators that are relatively weak include the business R&D intensity, the proportion of the population with tertiary education, the use of non-technological changes, and the introduction of new processes and products (at least those that are new to the firm). This chapter begins by discussing the aspects of innovation activity that are relatively weak. It then analyses the causes of these weaknesses, discusses reforms that are being made to attenuate them and suggests directions in which the reforms could be taken further.

A Dutch paradox

The Netherlands performs well in knowledge creation: scientific publications *per capita* are 6th highest in the OECD (Figure 5.1) and the citation impact is high at 25% above the worldwide citation average.[2] However, innovation activity, which entails the development and application of new knowledge in new products and/or processes, appears to be only mediocre. According to the European Innovation Scoreboard (EIS) Summary Innovation Index, which brings together 22 indicators considered to reflect innovation activity (Box 5.1), innovation activity in the Netherlands ranks 12th out of the 20 high-income countries for which the index has been calculated (Figure 5.2). Although the Netherlands ranks slightly above the EU15 average, it is far below the leaders. Along with Norway, the Netherlands ranks 6 places lower on innovation activity than on the scientific publications score, the largest fall in ranking between these two indicators (Table 5.1). This performance represents a paradox because rankings for scientific publications and innovation activity are in general highly correlated.

This chapter identifies the areas in innovation activity where Dutch performance is weak and makes recommendations to improve performance and thereby reduce the gap between knowledge creation and innovation activity. To focus the discussion, factor analysis[3] (see Annex 5.A1 for details) has been used to determine which of the EIS indicators are related to the same underlying phenomena, with the other indicators being set aside. Ten of the EIS indicators are highly related to each other and seem to reflect *knowledge development*.[4] The Dutch score on these indicators is high for European Patent Office (EPO) high-tech patent applications and public R&D expenditure as a share of GDP but below average on the proportion of the population with tertiary education and business expenditures on R&D as a percentage of GDP (see Annex 5.A1, Table 5.A1.4). Four additional indicators[5] are related to each other and mostly appear to reflect *knowledge application*. The Netherlands scores relatively poorly on all four of these indicators, pointing to weaknesses in implementing organisational change and in introducing new products and/or processes (see Annex 5.A1, Table 5.A1.5).

Figure 5.1. **Scientific articles per million population, 2001**[1]

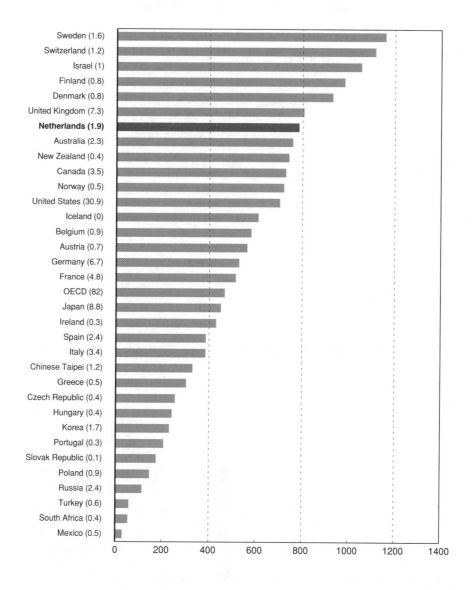

1. Data in parenthesis represent the country share in total world scientific articles in 2001.
Source: OECD (2005a), *OECD Science, Technology and Industry: Scoreboard 2005.*

Improving knowledge development

Increasing business R&D expenditure

Business R&D intensity is relatively low

Business R&D intensity in the Netherlands is 1.0% of GDP (Figure 5.3), which is low in comparison with both the EU15 average (1.3% of GDP) and the OECD average (1.5% of GDP) and far behind the leaders. Moreover, while R&D intensity has increased markedly in most OECD countries over the last two decades, especially in a number of other small European

Box 5.1. **Indicators and weights for the 2004 EIS Summary Innovation Index (SII)***

Indicator	Weight	Indicator	Weight
1.1. S&E	1.0	3.1. SMEs innovating in-house	1.0
1.2. Work pop with 3rd education	1.0	3.2. SMEs innovation co-operation	1.0
1.3. Lifelong learning	1.0	3.3. Innovation expenditures	1.0
1.4. Employment med/hi-tech manufacturing	1.0	3.4. SMEs using non-tech change	1.0
1.5. Employment high-tech services	1.0	4.1. High-tech venture capital	1.0
2.1. Public R&D expenditure	1.0	4.2. Early stage venture capital	1.0
2.2. Business R&D expenditure	1.0	4.3.1. New-to-market products	1.0
2.3.1. EPO high-tech patents	0.5	4.3.2. New-to-firm products	1.0
2.3.2. USPTO high-tech patents	0.5	4.4. Internet access (composite indicator)	1.0
2.4.1. EPO patents	0.5	4.5. ICT expenditures	1.0
2.4.2. USPTO patents	0.5	4.6. Value added high-tech manufacturing	1.0
		Total	20.0

* Detailed descriptions of these indicators in Hollanders and Arundel, 2004 Country rankings can be found in Annex 5.A1, Tables 5.A1.4 and 5.A1.5.

Figure 5.2. **European Innovation Scoreboard Summary Index in 2004**

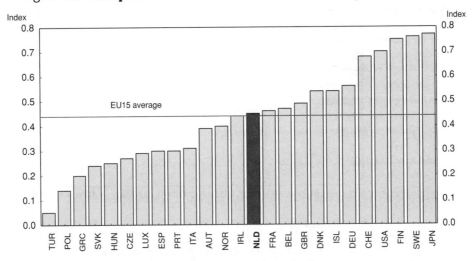

Source: European Commission, European Innovation Scoreboard 2004 database.

countries, R&D spending in the Netherlands has been stable, remaining at its low starting point (Table 5.2).

About 60% of the shortfall compared with the OECD average is related to the industry structure (Erken and Ruiter, 2005, Table 12.1): R&D extensive sectors are relatively large in the Netherlands. As far as low business R&D expenditure is attributable to specialisation in sectors that are R&D extensive, there is not much that can be done about it in the near term. However, in the longer-term, success in innovation and related policies could contribute to shifting the Netherlands' competitive advantage towards more R&D intensive sectors. The remaining shortfall can be mainly attributed to lower inward R&D

Table 5.1. **Ranking for scientific publications and EIS Summary Innovation Index**[1]

	Scientific publications Per million inhabitants	EIS Summary Innovation Index	Difference in ranking
Austria	12	15	–3
Belgium	9	10	–1
Denmark	4	7	–3
Finland	3	3	0
France	11	11	0
Germany	10	6	4
Greece	18	16	2
Iceland	13	8	5
Ireland	15	13	2
Italy	17	17	0
Japan	14	1	13
Luxembourg	20	20	0
Netherlands	**6**	**12**	**–6**
Norway	8	14	–6
Portugal	19	19	0
Spain	16	18	–2
Sweden	2	2	0
Switzerland	1	5	–4
UK	5	9	–4
US	7	4	3
Spearman's rank correlation 0.734, t = 4.58			

1. Table includes only the countries from Figure 5.1 for which EIS data are available.

Source: OECD (2005a), *OECD Science, Technology and Industry: Scoreboard*, European Innovation Scoreboard and our calculations.

investments by foreign firms (*i.e.*, R&D expenditure of foreign affiliates) in the Netherlands (adjusted for the openness of the economy) in relation to total R&D (Figure 5.4).[6] In 2001, approximately one-quarter of total private R&D expenditure in the Netherlands came from foreign affiliates. Given the open character of the Dutch economy, however, one would expect the foreign component in total private R&D in the Netherlands to amount to 50% (instead of 25%). This observation is strengthened by looking at FDI in general (see Figure 5.5). The figure clearly shows that, adjusted for the openness of the economy, the Netherlands performs quite well in attracting FDI in general. The main problem, therefore, is the R&D component within total inward FDI, which is, as already concluded, too low. This suggests that private R&D could be increased by improving the R&D climate – especially for inward R&D.

Factors to improve the climate for business R&D

Based on a review of empirical results from the economic literature, a field study and an econometric analysis based on macroeconomic data, Erken, Kleijn and Lantzendörffer (2005) conclude that the most important location factors for inward R&D activities are the availability of highly-skilled (science and engineering) personnel, international accessibility, the quality of knowledge institutions, the value added of foreign firms, the stock of private R&D capital and the cooperation between firms and knowledge institutes (Figure 5.6). Of these factors, the Netherlands only scores below average on private R&D capital stock and cooperation between firms and knowledge institutes. Improving performance on such co-operation would strengthen both inward and domestic R&D.

Figure 5.3. **Business enterprise sector expenditure on R&D**

Per cent of GDP, 2003 or latest available year

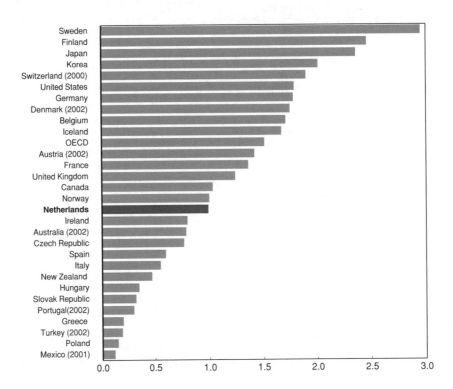

Source: OECD (2005b), *Main Science and Technology Indicators*, 2005:1.

Table 5.2. **Long-term developments in business R&D intensity**

Percentage of GDP

	1981	2003
Netherlands	0.95	0.99
Belgium	1.00	1.71
Austria	0.61	1.42[1]
Denmark	0.53	1.75[1]
Finland	0.64	2.46
EU15	1.04	1.25
OECD	1.28	1.51

1. 2002.

Source: OECD (2005b), *Main Science and Technology Indicators*, 2005:1.

Similarly, strengthening performance on other location factors, notably the availability of highly-skilled personnel, which is ranked as the most important location factor, would also promote both inward and domestic R&D. The low share of tertiary graduates in younger age groups relative to the share in other advanced countries (see below) and the low share of science and engineering graduates in total graduations (see below) raise concerns about the future availability of highly skilled personnel in the Netherlands.

Figure 5.4. **Inward R&D as a share of total R&D in relation to openness of the economy**

2001

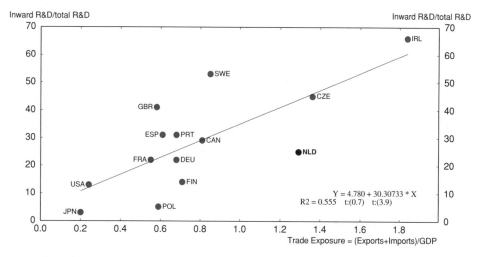

Source: OECD (2005c), OECD Economic Outlook 78 database; Erken and Ruiter (2005).

Figure 5.5. **FDI in relation to openness of the economy**

1990-2003 average

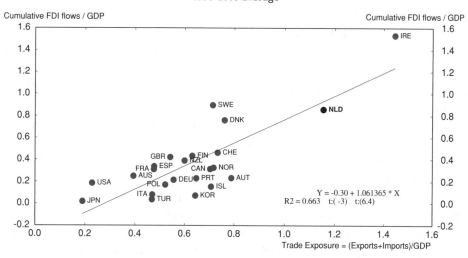

Source: OECD, (2005c), OECD Economic Outlook 78 database, OECD (2005d), *Factbook 2005: Economic, Environmental and Social Statistics.*

Enhance co-operation between knowledge institutions and firms

Co-operation between knowledge institutions and firms is vital for applying new knowledge in innovative products and processes. In the Netherlands, the share of innovative enterprises that participates in partnerships with universities or research institutes is comparatively low (Ministry of Economic Affairs (MEA) and Ministry of Education, Culture and Science (MECS), 2004a, Figure 5.6). Research institutes are a relatively important source of information for innovative enterprises but not higher education institutes (MEA and MECS, 2004, Figure 5.7). Moreover, university spin-off activity is comparatively weak (MEA and MECS, 2004, Figure 5.8) and public research

Figure 5.6. **Performance of the Netherlands on the important location factors for foreign R&D investments**

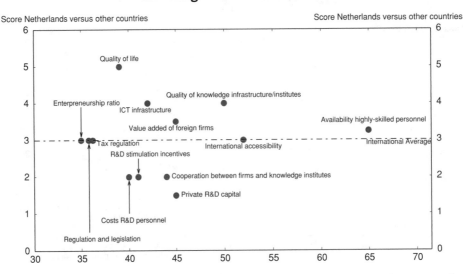

Source: Erken, Kleijn and Lantzendörffer (2005).

organisations (PRO) own relatively few patents (Bongers, den Hertog, Vandeberg and Segers, 2003; Pain and Jaumotte, 2005). Furthermore, the Dutch patents of PRO (and businesses) seem to be less commercially exploited than in other countries (Bongers, den Hertog, Vandeberg and Segers, 2003).

It appears that universities are not given enough incentives to exploit their in-house knowledge and patents and have insufficient capabilities to commercialise their research. This may be related to university funding being mainly based on historical distributions, a lack of intellectual property rights (IPR) management skills in the public research domain, and salary scales that make incentive provision for technological transfer organisations (TTOs) difficult. A small step towards making university budgets more dependent on co-operation with firms in innovation activities is being taken by reallocating part of the university research budget (€ 100 million out of a total budget of € 2 billion) on the basis of the funds a university receives for research projects from the national research council (NWO) and third parties. It is still a matter of discussion if this is a sufficient step forward. The government has recently set-up a committee of external experts that will advise on this issue (the Chang committee). While universities have wide discretion to give incentives to staff to co-operate with firms in innovation projects, so far only a few universities have acted in this regard by implementing (on a small scale) the so-called tenure track system, in which researchers are given a clear career path with a corresponding income scale.

Another factor that may contribute to the limited use made of Dutch knowledge creation in business innovation is strong public sector demand for research in certain, predefined areas, which could crowd out possible public-private research networks. This conclusion is supported by evidence that the simultaneous presence of public authorities on the demand and supply side of the research market is leading to a distortion of resources away from private sector needs (Rensman, 2004). Low mobility of researchers between PRO and business enterprises also inhibits co-operation by limiting the development of personal networks and exchanges of tacit information.

In order to strengthen science-business linkages, a variety of institutions to support knowledge transfer has been set up (Box 5.2). These include the Innovation Platform (set-up in 2003), which comprises cabinet members and leading actors from PRO and business and proposes strategic plans to reinforce the Dutch knowledge economy, and four Leading Technology Institutes (Technologische Top Instituten, TTI, created in 1997), which are virtual institutes for public-private co-operation on fundamental and strategic research in applied sciences. Through the TTI, the Dutch government is trying to improve – in cooperation with specific universities – innovative capacity and competitive strength in industries that draw on knowledge in certain areas (telematics, agro-food, metals, and polymers). The TTI have contributed significantly to improving public-private partnerships for research and innovation (OECD, 2004). In addition, more weight is to be given to demand-driven financing of the applied research institutes (TNO) and large technology institutes (GTI).[7] To realise a joint agenda on research and innovation activities, the government has established two coordination organisations ("regie-organen") in the fields of genomics and ICT. Improving co-operation between such companies and PRO should be a priority. In this regard, a new policy instrument (the smart mix) will be launched in 2006 that provides for programmes to enhance focus and mass in excellent basic research and social and economic valorisation of this research. These programmes are to be run by consortia of organisations from the research sector, firms and social organisations.

Measures have also been taken to strengthen PRO-business interactions through greater spin-off activity. Existing instruments to support the creation of technology-based start-ups were streamlined into one programme in 2004, the TechnoPartner Action Programme. In the context of this programme, the TechnoPartner Seed Facility aims to stimulate the lower end of the Dutch venture capital market so that high-tech start-ups, including spin-offs from public institutes, have adequate access to capital. The other programme that bears directly on PRO-business linkages is the TechnoPartner Knowledge Exploitation Subsidy Arrangement (SKE), which encourages business to use scientific knowledge created by publicly financed researchers. The other part of the TechnoPartner Action Programme is the TechnoPartner Platform, which aims to stimulate technology start-ups by promoting entrepreneurship (see below) and identifying barriers that can be removed. In this respect, as noted above, Dutch universities need to become more professional in applying for patents and to transfer them more smoothly to start-ups (MEA and MECS, 2004, p. 96). Universities should be allowed to earmark funds to create facilities aimed at improving the management of their patent pool. It would also help if universities and other PRO were able to benefit from a limited international grace period for patenting (granting patents even for publicly available research not older than one year), thereby mitigating the dilemma between the desire to publish quickly and the novelty requirement for patenting.

The Casimir programme, which is based on the Marie Curie- and the French Cifre Schemes, has been established to foster mobility of researchers between PROs and the private sector and to make jobs in research more attractive. It gives subsidies (up to € 160 000 per project) for projects having three partners – a company, a university and an individual researcher. The programme is intended to enable academic researchers to participate in corporate R&D and industry researchers to participate in research at PRO. Project applications are considered by a cross-disciplinary assessment committee, possibly leading to cross-fertilisation. The resulting circulation of knowledge both between the public and the private sphere as well as across sectors is considered to be a pre-condition

Box 5.2. **Institutions to transfer knowledge**

Three major actors are present in the Dutch research sector to provide knowledge creation and transfer: The Netherlands Organisation for Applied Research (TNO); the Large Technological Institutes (GTI, Grote Technologische Institute); and the Leading Technological Institutes (TTI, Technologische Top Instituten).

The TNO comprises 14 specialised institutes that focus on quality of life, defence and public safety, advanced products, processes and systems, the natural and man-made environment, and ICT and services. There are currently 34 Knowledge Centres in which TNO and universities co-operate on specific themes and 50 university professors working part time at TNO. The objective of TNO is to translate scientific knowledge into applied knowledge that is useful for the private sector and government agencies. Through specific financing, the Ministry of Economic Affairs' contributions to TNO are made dependent on the extent to which the private sector is prepared to support TNO research projects. This is designed to promote more demand-driven strategic and applied research.

The GTIs (ECN, GeoDelft, MARIN, NLR, and WL/Delft Hydraulics) were set up to act as transfer institutes for the production of basic knowledge at universities and its application in society (MEA and MECS, 2004, p. 65). In the domain of aerospace, energy, hydraulics, geodesy and marine sciences, they have as their mission the transformation of scientific/ fundamental knowledge into applied knowledge for industry (and the government/public administration). The government provides basic funding, as well as financial means for research linked to specific technologies and projects. The amount of this targeted funding is linked to co-funding raised by the institutes for specific projects.

The TTIs (*Technologische Top Instituten* or Leading Technological Institutes), created in 1997 and supported by the Dutch government (it provides around one half of their funding) are aimed at improving the innovative capacity and competitive strength of industry in a number of selected fields. This is achieved through industry-relevant fundamental and strategic research of an excellent international standard, in institutional partnerships between industry and the public research infrastructure. Presently there are four institutes in operation:

- Telematica Institute (situated at the Twente University campus): aims to become industry's long-term research partner to foster business innovation in telematics within and across key players.

- Wageningen Centre of Food Sciences (WCFS; situated near Wageningen Agricultural University Research Centre): concentrates on pre-competitive research, on topics key to future competitiveness of the Dutch agro-food sector, linking food and biosciences/ biomedical research.

- Netherlands Institute for Metals Research (NIMR; situated at Delft Technical University): aims to achieve leadership in research and education in areas critical for the international competitiveness of the Dutch metals industry by means of cross-disciplinary research and training.

- Dutch Polymer Institute (DPI; situated at Eindhoven Technical University) has the mission to establish a leading technological institute in Europe in the area of polymer science and engineering, involving establishment of a fundamental knowledge base for industry, development of new industrial concepts and training of scientists and engineers.

for public-private spin-offs. It should ensure greater use of existing research potential both in the public and private sectors.

Interaction between PRO and business is also being strengthened through the distribution of knowledge vouchers to SMEs. These vouchers (of € 7 500 each) can be used to obtain available knowledge from universities or other research institutes. So far 100 vouchers have been issued. In March 2005 an extra of 400 vouchers have been issued and in October 2005 another 600. The cabinet plans to issue 3000 in 2006. Vouchers can also be used to obtain knowledge from large companies and knowledge institutes in Flandres and Northrein-Westphalia. Requests for vouchers that fulfil the qualifying conditions are randomly accepted – equally valid requests are satisfied in some cases and not in others. This feature of the scheme facilitates evaluation as there is no systematic difference between SMEs that won the lottery and those that lost. An evaluation of the first 100 vouchers (CPB, 2005a) concluded that eight out of ten companies would not have obtained knowledge from third parties without the voucher. Other instruments to improve cooperation between higher (vocational) education institutions and SMEs include: financial support for knowledge-development and knowledge-exchange projects of higher education and SMEs; and support for intermediaries between vocational education institutions and firms and for knowledge circles aimed at improving the external orientation of (higher) educational institutes – especially with regard to SMEs.

While science-industry linkages provide an important means for firms to access new knowledge provided by the public knowledge infrastructure, firm networking to share costs of knowledge creation and innovation – such as strategic alliances – both within the Netherlands and with foreign firms are important ways of generating and diffusing knowledge domestically and cross-country. These networks are usually slow to generate large benefits and may prove profitable only over the long-run, potentially constituting a reason for policy intervention. Dutch firms seem to lack experience and skills in innovation co-operation agreements, preferring instead to set up joint ventures for co-operative innovation projects (Duysters and De Man, 2003). This represents a major barrier to Dutch firms collaborating in innovation networks.

A number of institutions promote networking and cooperation. Syntens, an organisation funded by the Government, is actively involved in network activities for innovative SME's to stimulate cooperation and knowledge transfer. SenterNovem (agency of the MEA that implements innovation and sustainable development policies) is also active in the field of stimulating networking and organizing activities *e.g.* brokerage events. One of the major tasks of SenterNovem is to mediate and create links between and among firms and organisations in a specific field. Networking is also promoted by branch organisations, under the impact of the active role played by the Ministry of Economic Affairs. Further information facilities, sound management education and coordination efforts on behalf of chambers of commerce would help to foster such networks. Anti-trust law and merger control is not a barrier to the development of such networks as the Dutch competition authority (NMa) takes into account any impact of tight anti-trust regulation on a firm's capacity to enter into a collaboration agreement on innovation projects (article 6 of the Dutch Competition Act).

Rationalising instruments and organisations supporting innovation to enhance effectiveness

Over the years a plethora of instruments and organisations has been created in the Netherlands. This has led to concerns about the complexity and effectiveness of the system. In addition, high administrative costs tend to reduce the impact of financial support on business R&D – less of the budget remains to stimulate business R&D. The large number of – partly overlapping – instruments[8] and organisations[9] supporting innovation has resulted in high administrative costs. These are estimated to be 4%-8% for support for business R&D (Ministry of Finance, 2002). Costs tend to be higher for small specific instruments than for large generic instruments and can be very high for specific instruments supporting diffusion (up to 39%, *ibid.*).

The Ministry of Economic Affairs has taken several steps to address these concerns, including the integration of the various initiatives to foster the creation of technology-based start-ups in the TechnoPartner Action programme and the merging of the two agencies of the Ministry of Economic Affairs that implement policies on innovation and sustainable development (Senter and Novem). Most importantly, the Ministry of Economic Affairs sent a letter to Parliament in May 2005 on the radical renewal of financial instruments (MEA, 2005). The new setup of instruments entails a reduction in the large number of instruments directed at the stimulation of R&D and innovation and a new organisational set up for the implementation of these instruments (Box 5.3). It aims at increased flexibility and customisation, fewer instruments with more coherence, fewer and more accessible helpdesks and lower acquisition costs and administrative burdens. An accessible and transparent basic package provides entrepreneurs with information and capital. The focus is primarily on entrepreneurs that want to innovate, export and/or engage in overseas investment. In addition, a related programme-based package offers the possibility to focus innovation resources on a limited number of fields in which the Netherlands can excel. The programme – based approach also aims at improving science-industry linkages and focus in innovation policy.

The progressive incorporation of a number of existing instruments into an "innovation omnibus",[10] a legal framework on the basis of which a wide range of initiatives can be supported financially will make possible custom-made stimulation of public-private initiatives through the programme package.[11] It is envisaged that businesses and knowledge institutions will initiate innovation programmes themselves, setting out aims, activities and required resources. Each programme is intended to be unique: the participants will decide the most suitable form of organisation and action needed to reach the objectives. The best programme proposals submitted to the MEA may qualify for financial or other support that is tailored to the needs of the organisation concerned. This reform is part of a change of policy direction in the Netherlands entailing a shift from generic towards specific support for innovation (Box 5.4). However, a lack of information on external benefits of specific projects increases the risk for capture. This risk could be reduced by introducing strict sunset clauses and consulting external experts.

Increasing financial support for innovation

The current government has increased expenditure on innovation considerably, reflecting the priority it gives to the knowledge economy. In its government agreement, the cabinet decided to increase the annual budget for knowledge and innovation by € 700 million (3.5% of the budget for knowledge and innovation) to foster public-private

Box 5.3. **Renewal of financial instruments**

The Ministry of Economic Affairs is changing the design of its financial instruments because the existing instruments lack flexibility and coherence, funds are spread very thinly and there are too many different helpdesks. To address these problems, it will introduce a widely accessible basic package and a programme-based package (MEA, 2005). The fiscal incentive for innovation (WBSO) is not included in this renewal, because the authorities consider this fiscal incentive to be a general macroeconomic framework condition within an attractive fiscal climate. Recently, these plans were adopted by Parliament.

The basic package consists of two elements: information and advice; and capital. This package contains the generic innovation instruments (*e.g.*, innovation vouchers), (risk) capital instruments and intermediaries. A range of organisations provide the entrepreneur with information and advice: SenterNovem; Syntens; The Netherlands Patents Centre; the EVD (the Netherlands Foreign Trade Agency); and the Chambers of Commerce. The number of helpdesks will be reduced and accessibility improved. In May 2005 a "front office" was set up for two agencies SenterNovem and EVD, providing the entrepreneur with a single point of contact. An "Entrepreneurs Forum" will be set up in each region, where the Chambers of Commerce and Syntens will jointly offer their services. The front office will be connected in 2005 to a customer-orientated, digital source of assistance where entrepreneurs can find information on legislation and regulations from all relevant government authorities.

The programme package aims at achieving top performance in a number of areas where the Netherlands can really excel in the future. Currently, funds are divided up among a large number of projects in a variety of areas. It is expected that significant benefits could be achieved if support were more focused. Therefore, a number of financial instruments will be incorporated into an "innovation omnibus" to support a limited number of strategic areas of innovation. Areas are chosen in close collaboration with the business sector, knowledge institutions, other departments and government authorities, politicians and the Innovation Platform. The selection will be based on the (potential) benefits for the Dutch economy and contribution to future innovations. Innovation programmes will be developed and implemented within these areas. Businesses and knowledge institutions will take the initiative to develop these programmes, setting out aims, activities and contributing to the required resources. The programmes therefore rely on the organisational skills and financial commitment of the field. The implementing organisation actively takes the lead in this process and tries to exploit opportunities and solve problems together with the parties. The MEA will offer the parties involved a customised package of support. This package could include support in the form of foreign missions, legislation and regulations and interventions with other government authorities, but it could also involve a direct financial contribution to projects and programmes.

A budget will also be made available for "challengers". Projects will be included in this category that do not fit in programmes, but nevertheless have considerable potential. Possible ways of encouraging these "challengers" could be subsidies or credit facilities for high-risk projects to develop new products, processes, software or services. These challengers are expected to become an important resource for finding new themes.

Box 5.4. **More specific support**

The Dutch government is moving more of its support for innovation towards specific instruments.[1] This is being done because the authorities consider that the external benefits of the relatively small Dutch budget for R&D would be greater by focusing support on specific fields that are most important to the economy. By the end of 2003, € 800 million had been invested from the FES (Economic Structure Enhancing Fund) in strengthening the knowledge infrastructure (increase public-private cooperation and focus). These funds have been spent in the five areas retained for focus: genomics (life sciences), ICT, nanotechnology, spatial planning and durable system innovation. The first three were also identified as national research priorities by the Ministry of Education Culture and Sciences (2003). The plans for renewal of financial instruments by the Ministry of Economic Affairs mentioned above consist of a basic package of information, advice and capital facilities for all entrepreneurs and a programme-based package partly subsidising specific areas. However, within the new setting of financial instruments, the generic instruments aimed at stimulating business R&D (WBSO) and innovation (innovation vouchers) will continue to have a relatively large share within the total innovation budget (over two-thirds) of the MEA. With regard to specific support, the current priorities are ICT and sustainable energy. The MEA has also launched three pilot programmes on: high tech systems and materials; water; and food and flowers. These themes were selected by the Innovation Platform after a bottom-up consultation of all parties.

The Ministry of Education, Culture and Sciences has selected its priorities based on the importance of these fields for future scientific and economic development. However, many countries have chosen comparable research priorities. Hence marginal returns may be low. The MEA has chosen its priorities in collaboration with others, based on the perceived advantages for the Dutch economy. However, it is not clear whether sectors that have the largest advantage will offer the highest external benefits. Although there is some overlap, there seems to be room for improving the cooperation of the Ministry of Economic Affairs and the Ministry of Education, Culture and Sciences with respect to selecting key areas.

While targeted support for innovation could increase external benefits compared with generic support (it may be reasonable to conclude that research in certain areas is likely to have wide ranging applications), there is a risk of government failure. As little is known about the external benefits of specific support, it could end up going to fields or projects with relatively low external benefits. Moreover, the increased opportunities for rent-seeking behaviour with specific support raise the probability of this outcome occurring. To limit this risk, the MEA selects programmes through a bottom-up process which reveals more information. In view of these uncertainties, a cautious approach in shifting towards specific innovation support is warranted, which is the approach being adopted by the government. The programme-based approach of the MEA will only amount to approximately € 0.2-€ 0.25 billion and partly involves a shift from subsidising specific activities (*e.g.*, co-operation) to funding specific fields. This compares with a total budget for supporting innovation other than that going to universities (€ 2 billion) and the NWO (Netherlands Organisation for Scientific Research) and KNAW (Royal Netherlands Academy of Arts and Sciences) (€ 0.5 billion) of € 1.5 billion, which is presently equally divided between specific- and generic innovation policies; the WBSO (generic tax-incentive on private R&D) is the largest individual scheme, amounting to € 0.4 billion.[2] The government has little influence over the way universities spend their (main part of (university)) research funding.

1. In 2003 the Dutch Advisory Council for Science and Technology Policy (AWT) advised the government to shift its innovation policy towards "backing the winners"; in close cooperation with scientists and the business community it should build on existing and potential strengths of the Dutch economy (AWT, 2003: backing winners). Reacting to this, the Royal Netherlands Economic Association (KvS) advised that government should instead "back the challengers"; to foster innovation, existing strongholds of power have to be challenged and knocked down (KvS 2004: Innovatie in Nederland).

2. These rough estimates are based on "Wetenschapsbudget 2004", "IBO Technologiebeleid" and "*www.NWO.nl*".

research cooperation, among other things. In addition, the already substantial WBSO tax breaks were extended further, especially for SMEs (an increase of € 100 million), innovation vouchers for SMEs were introduced and an experiment with a small business innovation and research initiative (SBIR) has been started. During Easter, the cabinet reached an additional agreement *Paasakkoord* (Easter agreement) to spend part of the windfall gains from increased gas prices on strengthening the knowledge infrastructure, *e.g.*, innovation vouchers, high quality research (nanotechnology, biotechnology, pharmaceuticals, ICT) and large research facilities. Given the estimated external benefits of business R&D (OECD, 2003c), a case can be made for increasing public support for business R&D. However, this case is independent of gas windfalls, as should be decisions about the appropriate level of such support. Moreover, the effectiveness of different instruments to support innovation should be taken into account.

Attracting foreign scientists and engineers and encouraging those already in the Netherlands to stay

Increasing the number of scientists and engineers would make the Netherlands more attractive for both inward and domestic R&D. The fastest way to increase the availability of such personnel is to increase immigration of persons with such skills. This would also help to address complaints that have been made by foreign investors in the Netherlands that they have had difficulty in bringing good personnel to the country even in cases where they have been unable to find suitable personnel in the Netherlands (Erken, Kleijn and Lantzendörffer, 2005, p. 10). The Netherlands has not been very successful in attracting and retaining foreign human resources in science and technology (HRST) (OECD, 2005e, Figure A.1.1). Not only are HRST immigration flows relatively low, but such immigrants also tend not to stay in the Netherlands, regarding it as stepping stone to other destinations. In order to increase entry of "knowledge migrants"[12] from outside the EU, the government recently took steps to facilitate their entry. It established a single point of contact, shorter procedures and limited levies for knowledge immigrants, as recommended by the Innovation Platform (IP, 2003). The government has expressed its intention to consider further steps to facilitate such immigration.[13]

Another means by which countries seek to attract foreign HRST is to attract foreign students and enable them to work in the country after completing their studies. Only 4% of students in the Netherlands are foreigners, compared with 18-19% in the leading countries, Australia and Switzerland (OECD, 2005e, Table C.3.1). Moreover, less than 20% of foreign students study science and engineering in the Netherlands, compared with more than 30% in a number of countries (including Australia and Switzerland) (OECD, 2005e, Figure C3.4). Following successful completion of a higher education programme (HBO/WO-level) in the Netherlands, non-EU graduates have three months to find a position that qualifies them as knowledge migrants. Otherwise, they must leave the country. The authorities should give graduates more time to find a position that qualifies them as knowledge migrants before obliging them to leave the country. More flexibility as to what constitutes a knowledge worker should also be introduced as science and engineering graduates do not always have high earnings relative to other knowledge workers.

The Netherlands also appears to have some difficulty in retaining highly qualified HRST. It has one of the highest numbers of science and engineering PhDs (normalised for the home country population) working in the United States among non-English speaking countries (Figure 5.7). Other European countries are also subject to this brain drain, with

Figure 5.7. **Non-US OECD citizens with science and engineering doctorates in the United States**

As a percentage of the home country working age population in 1999

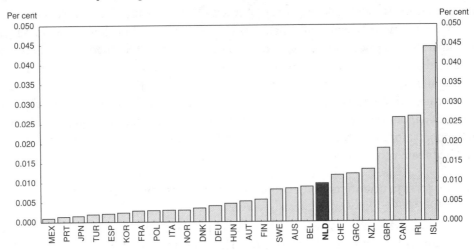

Source: OECD (2005a), *OECD Science, Technology and Industry: Scoreboard.*

France having recently become the major European supplier of such personnel (MERIT, 2003). The main reasons cited for EU-born science and engineering PhDs to go to or stay in the United States and for US-born such persons to return home are a broader scope of activities, better access to leading edge technologies, better career advancement opportunities and better access to R&D funding in the United States (*ibid.*). Concerning career advancement opportunities, a problem in the Netherlands is that tenured baby boomers occupy many posts (as in the United States) and rarely move (in contrast to the United States). According to the authorities, Dutch researchers are also hampered in their work by having to spend much more time arranging funding – especially within universities – for research projects than do their US counterparts. The Chang Committee that will advise on performance-based university funding (see below) will also present proposals on reducing the administrative burden of obtaining funding. Given the increasing internationalisation of R&D activities, further action to increase the attractiveness of the Dutch research climate seems to be paramount. This would include simplifying funding procedures within universities, developing centres of excellence, increasing staff mobility and increasing performance-based funding without too much administrative burden.

Increasing the flow of science and engineering graduates

The low flow of science and engineering graduates in the Netherlands poses a threat to the country's capacity to maintain the stock of scientists and engineers near the OECD average and hence to its attractiveness for R&D activities. While in principle the low domestic inflow of such personnel could be compensated for through immigration, the Netherlands has not had much success to date in attracting such immigrants and international competition for them is becoming fiercer. The low share of science and engineering graduates in the 20-29 age-group mainly reflects the low share of these disciplines in total graduations (Figure 5.8). Poor career prospects in science and engineering jobs relative to those in management encourage students to pursue studies in

Figure 5.8. **Science and engineering degrees as a percentage of total new degrees**
2000

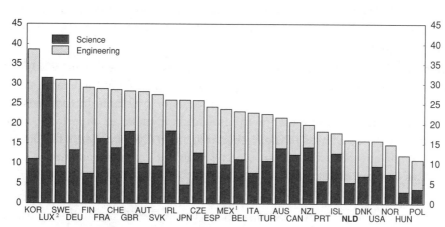

1. Excludes advanced research programmes.
2. Excludes tertiary-A second degree programmes and advanced research programmes.
Source: OECD (2003), *OECD Science, Technology and Industry: Scoreboard.*

economics, law and business, which give a better foundation for such careers than science and engineering. In addition, science and engineering studies are perceived by students as being uninteresting, difficult and entailing a heavy workload. All of these factors appear to have a stronger effect on women than on men. Indeed, the increase in the share of females in total graduations has contributed to a reduction in the share of science and engineering graduates in total graduations in the past 25 years; the share of S&E graduates in total graduates has not changed for either males or females (CPB, 2005b).

The government is aiming to increase the domestic supply of scientists and engineers by 2010 and beyond though the "Deltaplan". Education in science and technology from primary schools to universities is to be made more pupil-orientated to attract a wider and more diverse range of young people, including more females. At the same time, government is working together with business to give younger people a better perspective on scientific and technological careers. A variety of measures is being taken in this respect.[14] These measures will need to be carefully evaluated as they could prove costly in relation to the small number of S&E graduates that end up in R&D work because other professions are more attractive financially (CPB, 2005b). The "Deltaplan" also aims at increasing the attractiveness of research jobs. In addition, there are a number of policy initiatives to enlarge the influx of young talented researchers, including: the Innovation Research Incentive Scheme (which from 2005 also includes ASPASIA, a scheme oriented to women); and a Netherlands Organisation for Scientific Research (NWO)-programme oriented to persons from ethnic minorities.

Increasing foreign direct investment

As noted above, the FDI intensity of the Dutch economy in relation to its openness is average (see Figure 5.5). Some countries – Ireland, Sweden and Denmark – have considerably higher FDI intensity in relation to openness, suggesting that there is scope to do better in the Netherlands. Doing so would raise R&D inflows and hence R&D intensity. Following a decline in world economic growth and stagnation of the Dutch economy, FDI inflows in the Netherlands have decreased since 2000, as they have in most OECD countries (UNCTAD, 2004). However, surveys of foreign managers conducted by the MEA (2004) and Ernst&Young (2005) also suggest that the attractiveness of the Netherlands for FDI inflows has declined even abstracting from the business cycle; E&Y concludes, nevertheless, that the Netherlands remains attractive for certain types of FDI, notably European Headquarters.

Among the policy areas that impact on FDI patterns (Nicoletti *et al.*, 2003a), there is room for improvement in barriers to entrepreneurship, notably in the licence and permit system – which also is mentioned as one of the major problems in the questionnaire conducted by the MEA. Labour market reforms also could make an important contribution to increasing the attractiveness of the Netherlands for FDI. Respondents to both the MEA and Ernst&Young questionnaires regard Dutch labour market arrangements – *e.g.*, EPL and working time – as very unattractive.

Improving transport infrastructure – length of motorways and number of aircraft departures per capita –, which is below average among OECD countries (Nicoletti *et al.*, 2003, Annex 2, Table A2.10), and/or reducing road congestion (there were complaints about this in the MEA Survey) would also help to attract FDI. Implementing road pricing, as recently recommended by the *Platform Anders Betalen voor Mobiliteit*, (2005) (Platform Paying for Mobility in a Different Way)[15] – would help in this regard. The government has decided to implement road pricing in 2012.

Finally, the Netherlands, in co-operation with continental European countries, has made substantial progress over the past decade in reducing bilateral corporate tax wedges on cross-border activities of foreign affiliates, making the Netherlands a fiscally more attractive FDI destination. In 2001, the position of the Netherlands on the effective average tax rate (EATR)[16] was relatively favourable – slightly lower than the OECD average (Nicoletti *et al.*, 2003, Annex 1, figure 18). This seems to be in line with the results of the MEA survey, where respondents described the Dutch tax system as being reasonable. In 2005, the government reduced the corporate income tax rate from 34.50% to 31.50%, with the aim of further reducing it to 30.00% by 2007. The Dutch authorities recently announced a more ambitious plan to reduce the corporate tax rate to 26.9% by 1 January 2007.

Increasing the proportion of the population with tertiary education

The share of tertiary graduates in the Dutch population (25-64) is the same as the OECD average (OECD, 2005e, Table A1.3a) but ranks 12th amongst the 20 high-income countries included in the European Innovation Scoreboard (see Annex 5.A1, Table 5.A1.4, first column). This relatively unfavourable position for a high income country is likely to deteriorate as the proportion of tertiary graduates in the population aged 25-34 years is below the OECD average (Figure 5.9). Concomitantly, the increase in tertiary attainment as younger cohorts replace older ones will be smaller than on average in OECD countries.

The below-average proportion of tertiary graduates among the young is largely explained by the absence of differentiation in the supply of tertiary education. While enrolment of students in tertiary A (mainly theoretical programmes preparing for research and high-skill professions) programmes is at about the OECD-average, the absence of shorter (two or three-years) tertiary vocational programmes explains low enrolment in such programmes and brings down total average enrolment. The low degree of differentiation in the supply of tertiary education is also evident from fixed tuition fees,

Figure 5.9. **Population that has attained tertiary education**[1]

2003, per cent of age group

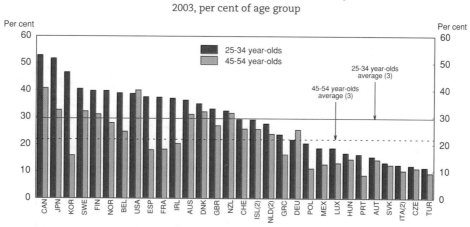

1. Tertiary education is defined as tertiary type A and advanced research programmes and tertiary type B education.
2. Data refers to 2002.
3. Unweighted average.

Source: OECD (2005e), *Education at a Glance.*

relatively long duration of programmes[17] and high barriers to entry for new suppliers of tertiary education.

Lower incentives for higher education institutions in the Netherlands to increase entry of students than in other OECD countries may also contribute to relatively low tertiary attainment. Funding of higher education is only partly based on performance in terms of input or output – in the university sector almost 40% of funding for education is not based on performance (CPB and CHEPS, 2001). Although a thorough international comparison is not available, it seems that countries that use performance based funding to a larger extent also perform better in terms of participation. This seems to be the case in Sweden (funding based entirely on number of students and number of study credits achieved by students) and the United States (performance-based funding and a high share of private funding by students) (CHEPS, 2001), while in Denmark the share of tertiary graduates in the 25-34 age group has increased markedly since the introduction of the taximeter model (funding entirely based on passed exams by students) in 1992; from 19% in 1991 to 31% in 2002.

As in many OECD countries, a steep increase in the number of students since the 1960s and cutbacks in the government budget in the 1980s has led to a marked decline in public expenditure per student (Figure 5.10). Currently, expenditure per student – relative to GDP per capita – is below the OECD average (Table 5.3) and is likely to decrease if entry rates rise – as total expenditure is more or less fixed, given the concerns over the government budget. Together with a relatively low extent of performance based funding, this factor could discourage higher education institutions from actively trying to increase entry rates.

The government is currently examining whether to introduce shorter tertiary vocational programmes. The CINOP (Centre for the Innovation of Education and Training) supported such an initiative in a recently published report commissioned by the Ministry of Education (CINOP, 2005). These programmes are expected to fill a demand – from students as well as the labour market – and, based on experience in other countries, – are expected to increase participation in higher education. A notable example in this regard is Finland, where higher education enrolment rates doubled between 1990 and 2000 following the creation of a new polytechnic sector that was differentiated in terms of

Figure 5.10. **Real public expenditure per student**
At 1960 prices

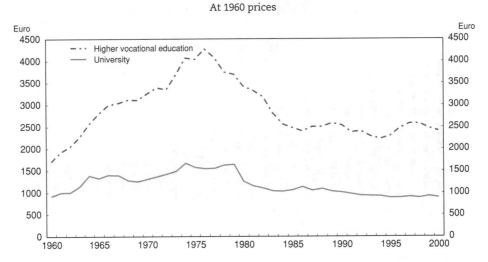

Source: Statistics Netherlands (CBS) Statline.

Table 5.3. **Annual expenditure on tertiary education
per student relative to GDP per capita (PPP US$)
in selected OECD countries, 2002**

The Netherlands	27
USA	51
Denmark	39
OECD	34
Sweden	28
Belgium	29
UK	31
Finland	26
France	27
Germany	25

Source: OECD (2005e), *Education at a Glance.*

duration of studies (shorter), content (more technically oriented, applied studies), governance (more employer, municipal, regional input), and financing (municipal, with local/regional in kind contribution of facilities).

The government also plans to extend performance-based funding in higher education. Students will receive "education rights" which they can spend at an institution for higher education; this will result in funding based on the number of students and the number of diplomas. In addition, a loan facility for tuition fees with income-contingent repayments will be introduced (MECS, 2004). A larger extent of performance based funding (i.e., funding per student and (to a lesser extent) per diploma) would increase the incentive to raise entry rates. To further foster the number of students receiving tertiary education, the government is currently experimenting with differentiating tuition fees and giving new institutions access to public education funding (MECS, 2005). More freedom in setting tuition fees and a more competitive environment could stimulate differentiation in quality and the development of tailor-made programmes. This might attract students who currently decide not to attend tertiary education and could reduce the number of drop outs. To receive public funding, all currently funded higher education institutions have to get approval for their new programmes from central government *(macro-doelmatigheidstoets)*. If the government deems that there are too many of a certain type of programme, it can withhold public funding. Although this might be prudent policy from a public expenditure point of view (*i.e.*, not financing programmes that have low benefits), it also limits room for entrants and competition because institutions offering a specific programme have an advantage over potential entrants and existing institutions working to offer the same programme. The government should rely more on the ability of students to choose the most beneficial programme and ease restrictions on access to public funding (at a minimum, government should provide funding for specific programmes through competition between existing and new institutions).

Enhancing application of new knowledge

As noted above, the Netherlands ranks poorly on the set of innovation indicators characterised as representing the application of new knowledge. Relatively few SMEs report making non-technological changes or introducing new products or processes either developed internally or in collaboration with other firms. Moreover, for all enterprises, sales of products new to the firm but not to the market represent a relatively low share of turnover. In addition, total innovation expenditures as a share of turnover, including not just expenditure on R&D but also on aspects related to applying new knowledge commercially – machinery and equipment linked to product and process innovation, acquisition of patents and licenses, industrial design, training and the marketing of innovations – is relatively low. Increasing product market competition, notably through lower barriers to entrepreneurship, and making social institutions such as labour-market regulation more compatible with non-technological change, could help to strengthen this aspect of innovation activity.

Strengthening science-industry linkages, as discussed above, could also enhance the use of knowledge in new products, services and processes. Similarly, the renewal of financial instruments by the Ministry of Economic Affairs (Box 5.3) could also help as it aims at improving information and advice services for entrepreneurs (including the promotion of networks). Such services may foster the application of knowledge and best-practices that are new to the firm. In addition, the application of knowledge – in *e.g.*, new products – can be part of an innovation programme that is supported by the Ministry of Economic Affairs' new instruments, although this aspect of the programme is not eligible for financial support. Other instruments to improve the linkages between firms and knowledge institutes, like the knowledge voucher scheme mentioned above, could also contribute to greater application of new knowledge.

Strengthening entrepreneurship and competition

Theoretically, the relation between the level of competition and the level of innovation is ambiguous. Although competition may increase the incentive to innovate (to try and escape from competition), Aghion *et al.*, (2002) argue that fierce competition may also hamper innovation by reducing its benefits, especially in "unlevelled" industries.[18] This would result in an inverted U relationship between competition and innovation, which they find in accordance with their data. However, the level of competition can be influenced by various factors and empirical work by the OECD suggests that less stringent product market regulation – which is one of them – favours innovation (Pain and Jaumotte, 2005). In addition, entrepreneurial activity has played a major role in radical innovation. Although it goes too far to claim that entrepreneurs are involved in all radical innovation and that all small businesses are radical innovators, Baumol (2003) shows that a lot of revolutionary breakthroughs in the United States have been made by small, independent innovators.

Competition intensity in the Netherlands seems to be moderate by international comparison. The Netherlands has a high degree of openness and an average score on the PMR index (see Chapter 4). Furthermore, the entry rate of firms (start-ups and new affiliates) is comparable to other OECD countries (Figure 5.11). On the other hand, exits are relatively low, which may be an indication of weak competitive forces. In addition, although the entry rate is comparable, the number of people setting-up or owning a young enterprise is below the international average (Figure 5.12). This might indicate that a large share of entrants consists of new affiliates of existing firms.

Figure 5.11. **Entry and exit rates in selected OECD countries, average 1989-1997**

Percentage of continuing firms, firms with at least one employee

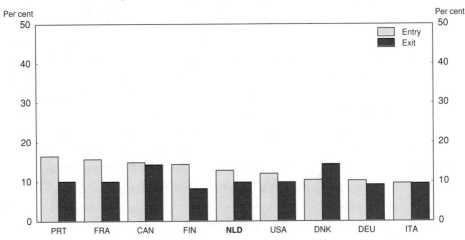

1. Denmark 1994-1997, France 1990-1996, Italy 1989-1993, USA 1989-1996.

Source: Scarpetta *et al.*, 2002.

Figure 5.12. **Total Entrepreneurial Activity (TEA) Index selected OECD countries**

Average 2001-2004

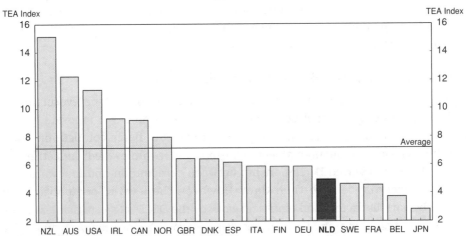

1. The number of people currently setting up a business or owning/managing one existing up to 3.5 years relative to the adult population 18-64 years.

Source: Global Entrepreneurship Monitor, 2004.

Like many other governments, the Dutch authorities aim at fostering an entrepreneurial culture through education. In 2000, the Ministry of Economic Affairs, in coordination with the Ministry of Education, launched a specific programme on Education for Entrepreneurship and introduced a subsidy scheme to promote the development of projects. From 2000 to 2003, more than 103 projects were developed for all education sectors (OECD, 2005f). Although education for entrepreneurship may foster awareness and entrepreneurial skills, risk-taking is to a large extent influenced by the institutional framework. Institutions influence the (expected) benefits of starting an (innovative) enterprise compared to the benefits of a regular job and, therefore, the willingness to make such a risky investment. Indeed, strict product market regulation – in particular administrative regulations on entrepreneurial activities – as well as strict EPL are found to have a negative impact on entry of small and medium sized firms (Scarpetta *et al.*, 2002). In this regard, barriers to entrepreneurship are relatively high in the Netherlands (see Chapter 4). This indicator includes procedures, *e.g.*, administrative and licences regulations, which constitute a much larger burden for SMEs than for larger companies and pose a barrier to entry. Although, the administrative burden – especially on SMEs – has been reduced considerably in the Netherlands, further action is needed to improve the licence and permit system and communication and simplification of rules.

Labour market regulations may pose a barrier to entry as well as to growth of enterprises. Strict hiring and firing rules make adjustments in the number of employees in case of success or a set-back more difficult and, therefore, hamper growth and experimentation by innovative SMEs. In addition, EPL raises the security of a regular job and reduces the incentive to start a company. Favourable social security benefits, *e.g.*, unemployment insurance and pensions, or other arrangements that are part of salaried employment can also add to the preference for a regular job. As mentioned in Chapter 3, the Netherlands has strict EPL on regular contracts and labour market regulations include a number of favourable arrangements for salaried employment concerning, for example, unemployment benefits, pensions and the legal right to adjust working hours. Increasing labour market flexibility, as recommended in chapter 3, would also help to strengthen entrepreneurship.

Another barrier to entry and experimentation may be posed by bankruptcy regulation, especially when the personal costs of bankruptcy are high. In the Netherlands, a bankrupt entrepreneur is sometimes liable for his debts for the rest of his life and may find it difficult to borrow money or even rent an apartment. This makes it very difficult to try to set-up a business a second time and reduces the incentive to start an enterprise or experiment in the first place. A new law on bankruptcy will be available at the end of 2005. As is the government's intention, this law should reduce the personal costs of bankruptcy and the options for a swift re-start of non-fraudulent bankrupts, *e.g.*, through offering a clean-slate by way of discharge. It is vital that this reform be implemented effectively and that the government ensures that potential entrepreneurs are adequately informed about it.

Promoting non-technical innovation

The Dutch government is concerned about a lack of non-technological innovation,[19] in particular a lack of social innovation, which concerns organisational change and competence management. This is seen as an important hindrance to organisations adapting new technologies and introducing new working practices that increase productivity. The lack of non-technological innovation in the Netherlands can be accounted for partly by the particular institutional setting on product and labour markets. In general, strong employment protection and seniority pay scales typical for centralised wage bargaining systems set incentives for firms to resort to internal workplace reorganisation and upgrading skills of their workforce, a strategy that may be of particular relevance for incremental innovation (Bassanini and Ernst, 2002). However, recent evidence points to the fact that in particular in service industries, reorganisation often takes place across firms more than within firms (Bosma and Nieuwenhuijsen, 2002). Consequently, tight employment protection will hamper external reorganisation, having a particularly strong impact on the service industries and their capacity for (non-) technological innovation. There is some indirect evidence for this thesis, based on the effect of employment protection on the service sector employment share: D'Agostino, Serafini and Ward (2005) find strong negative effects of EPL in particular in the telecommunications and financial sector, while the evidence is rather mixed for the impact of EPL on the overall service share (D'Agostino *et al.* (2005) find a significant negative effect, while Messina (2004) does not report such an effect).

In co-operation with the Ministry of Social Affairs and the Ministry of Education, the Ministry of Economic Affairs has set-up a task-force on social innovation, which recently presented its advice on how to foster social innovation. Although it identifies a role for government, *e.g.*, reducing the number of (detailed) regulations and procedures, social innovation is seen mainly as a responsibility of the social partners. Employers, employees and their representative organisations should give more priority to discussing changes in working practices and life-long learning and making less detailed sector-wide collective agreements. Although about two thirds of all the collective labour agreements pay at least some attention to social innovation and collective agreements have become less detailed in recent years, such agreements still leave a lot to be desired. Moreover, social innovation is not a priority at times of tension between social partners, as is presently the case. The Social Economic Council (SER) will investigate how social innovation can be made a more integral part of the agenda of the social partners in its middle-long-term advice, which is due at the end of 2005.

Conclusion

Innovation activity in the Netherlands only appears to be around the OECD average despite a strong performance in knowledge creation. The main weaknesses in innovation indicators are low business R&D intensity, the low (current and prospective) share of the population with tertiary education attainment and weak performance in applying new knowledge to new products and processes. Reforms to remedy these weaknesses are summarised in Box 5.5.

Box 5.5. **Policy recommendations to boost innovation activity**

Boost business R&D

A key factor in increasing the business R&D intensity is to make the Netherlands more attractive for R&D investment, including for inward R&D. To this end, the authorities should:

- continue to strengthen the linkages between firms and knowledge institutes to enhance the use of (scientific) knowledge in new products, processes and services;

- make university funding partly dependent on performance in diffusion of knowledge to firms to strengthen linkages between PRO and firms, as the government is considering doing;

- rationalise financial support for R&D activities, which is presently dispersed among a variety of agencies, so as to improve co-ordination;

- make greater use of evaluations of arrangements offering financial support to business R&D in policy development;

- take recent reforms to facilitate immigration of knowledge workers further by introducing a points system for immigrants, as in Canada, Australia and New Zealand, and by relaxing work permit rules for certain groups of non-employees, as is being considered;

- compete more aggressively for foreign PhD students in science and engineering and relax work permit rules to make it easier for them to stay in the Netherlands after graduation; and

- reduce the corporate tax rate to attract more FDI inflows, as planned.

Increase tertiary education

To increase the proportion of the population with tertiary education, the authorities should:

- provide funding for universities to offer short (two-year) courses, as in most other countries and as is being considered;

- increase the share of higher education funding based on performance in terms of inputs and outputs, as planned;

- differentiate tuition fees, as this will provide universities with an incentive to offer courses that are more attractive to students; and

- continue experiments with opening access to public funds for education services by allowing more private education suppliers to compete for public education funds so as to enhance the quality and diversity of courses offered.

Enhance the diffusion of innovation

To strengthen the application of new knowledge to new processes, more entrepreneurship, competition and social innovation are required. In this regard, the authorities should:

- continue education programmes in favour of entrepreneurship;

- reform bankruptcy law to reduce the personal costs of bankruptcy and increase options for a quick re-start of non-fraudulent bankrupts, as planned; and

- ease EPL on regular contracts (as recommended in Chapter 3) to facilitate workplace re-organisation in industries undertaking radical innovation.

Notes

1. The EC (European Commission (1995), 688) gives an expanded version of this definition: innovation is defined as "the renewal and enlargement of the range of products and services and the associated markets; the establishment of new methods of production, supply and distribution; and the introduction of changes in management, work organisation, and the working conditions and skills of the workforce".

2. Ministry of Economic Affairs and Ministry of Education, Culture and Science, 2004, Table 7.1.

3. "(Factor analysis aims) to explain the most of the variability among a number of observable random variables in terms of a smaller number of unobservable random variables called factors. The observed random variables are modelled as linear combinations of the factors, plus 'error' terms. The factor loadings (are) inferred from the data." *http://en.wikipedia.org/wiki/Factor_analysis*.

4. 1.2, 1.3, 1.5, 2.1, 2.2, 2.3.1, 2.3.2, 3.2, 4.2, and 4.6 (see Box 5.1 for definitions).

5. 3.1, 3.3, 3.4 and 4.3.2.

6. The sector composition effect on inward R&D is adjusted for by expressing inward R&D in relation to total R&D.

7. This follows the TNO/GTI evaluation that showed that more direct interaction between the demands of government, industry and society on the one hand, and the research institutions on the other was needed. The strategic plans of the TNO (2007-2010) will accommodate this structural reform of more demand driven research and finance.

8. The MEA lists 26 different instruments to support entrepreneurship, many of which are aimed at promoting innovation. In addition to the instruments listed in note 10, which will be absorbed into the new Innovation omnibus, current innovation instruments include: Knowledge Transfer Subsidy Scheme for Entrepreneurs; Knowledge Transfer Subsidy Scheme for Sector Organisations; Innovation Vouchers; and the Seed Facility (MEA, 2005, *Strong basis for delivering top performance – renewed instruments for entrepreneurs from the Ministry of Economic Affairs*). As noted above, the MEA plans to rationalise the list of support instruments.

9. Organisations involved in supporting innovation include a number of Ministries (of which the Ministry of Education, Culture and Sciences, and the Ministry of Economic Affairs are the most important), intermediary organisations that are responsible for executing support policies (*e.g.* SenterNovem and Laser) and public research institutions (*e.g.* NLR (National Aerospace Laboratory) and ECN (Energy Research Centre of the Netherlands)). In addition, a number of institutions advise the government on research and innovation policy: CPB (Netherlands Bureau for Economic Policy Analysis), SER (Social Economic Council), AWT (Advisory Council for Science and Technology Policy) and the Innovation Platform.

10. The Innovation Subsidy Scheme for Cooperative Projects (IS), Foundation for Technological Science (STW), Top Technological Institutes (TTI), Innovative Research Programmes (IOP), TechnoPartner, MEDEA/ITEA and possibly the MEA programme finance of The Netherlands Organisation for Applied Research (TNO) and the Large Technological Institutes (GTI) will be gradually incorporated in the omnibus. In order to ensure continuity in policy, a number of existing instruments will continue in their present form until the omnibus comes into effect on 1 January 2008.

11. This paragraph is based on MEA (2005).

12. A knowledge migrant is a migrant who comes to the Netherlands at the bequest of an employer (both private companies and public organisations) to carry out salaried employment and who earns a gross income of € 45 000 or more (gross income means the gross annual salary including payable income tax, employee's contributions and social security and pension premiums and holiday bonus, but excluding allowances, bonuses and non-monetary reimbursements. The amount is to be indexed each year). In the case of migrants under the age of thirty, the work permit obligation does not apply to incomes which correspond to the national health insurance limit (around € 32 600). The income criterion does not apply if the person concerned is to do a doctoral course at an education or research institution, nor to post-doctoral and university teachers aged less than thirty. Footballers, prostitutes and spiritual leaders or religious education teachers are excluded.

13. In particular, the government is investigating the introduction of a "points system" as in most English-speaking countries (MEA/MSAE, 2004: Agenda for Growth).

14. Measures include the following: 500 primary schools will start this year with a special programme for technology and science education with the help of industry (VTb), with a similar programme being planned for secondary education (JetNet); courses are to be made more attractive by

connecting science and engineering studies with problems in society and multi-disciplinary elements (which should be especially effective in attracting female students); and there are to be experiments with financial incentives in higher education to attract students to science and engineering courses.

15. This group was set up by the Ministers of Infrastructure and Finance

16. The EATR measures the wedge that a home country MNE expects to face when it invests in a host country, given tax requirements in both countries and the expected gross returns from the investment. It applies to an infra-marginal investment project that earns some economic rent, i.e. a project that earns after-tax pure profits.

17. The adoption of the Bologna framework, entailing Bachelors, Masters and PhD programmes with theoretical durations of three, five and eight years, respectively, should contribute to reducing actual course duration. Stronger incentives to complete courses within the theoretical duration (see below) would also help to reduce actual duration.

18. An industry is more "unlevel" (Aghion *et al.* also use the term "less neck-and-neck") if there's a large difference (in production costs) between the technological leader and its followers. .

19. Non-technological innovation, like workplace reorganisations, is not restricted to services but may find its origins mainly in service sector firms, such as consulting companies.

Bibliography

Aghion, P., Bloom, N., Blundell, R., Gri¢th, R. and Howitt, P. (2002), *Competition and Innovation: An Inverted U Relationship*, The Institute for Fiscal Studies, WP02/04.

Baumol, W.J. (2003), *Four Sources of Innovation and Stimulation of Growth in the Dutch Economy*, Ministry of Economic Affairs, The Hague.

Blöndal, S. S. Field, and Girouard, N. (2002), *Investment in human capital through post-compulsory education and training*, ECO/WKP(2002)19.

Bosma, N.S. and H.R. Nieuwenhuijsen (2002), *Bedrijfsdynamiek en groei*, Economisch Statistische Berichten, nr. 4349, pp. 172-174.

Bongers, F., P. Den hertog, R. Vandeberg and S. Segers (2003), *Naar een meetlat voor wisselwerking*, Dialogic, Utrecht.

CINOP (2005), *KORT EN GOED? Verkenning invoering korte programma's in het hoger beroepsonderwijs, [Short and Good? Survey on implementing short programmes in higher vocational education*, Dutch only], Den Bosch.

CHEPS (2001), *Public Funding of Higher Education: A Comparative Study of Funding Mechanisms in Ten Countries*, CHEPS-Higher education monitor, Enschede.

European Commission (1995), Green Paper on Innovation, COM(95)688.

CPB and CHEPS (2001), Higher education reform; getting the incentives right, The Hague.

CPB (2005a), *De effectiviteit van de innovatievoucher 2004 [The effectiveness of knowledge vouchers 2004*, Dutch only], CPB Document 95, The Hague.

CPB (2005b), *Scarcity of science and engineering students in the Netherlands*, CPB Document 92, The Hague.

D'Agostino, Antonello, Roberta Serafini and Melanie Ward (2005), *Sectoral explanations in Europe: The role of services*, unpublished ECB working paper.

Duysters, G. And Ard-Pieter de Man (2003), *De positie van Nederlandse bedrijven in innovatienetwerken [The position of Dutch companies in innovationnetworks*, Ducth only], Ministry of Economic Affairs, The Hague.

Ernst&Young (2005), The Netherlands...taking care of the future: Netherlands Attractiveness survey 2005, August 2005.

Erken, H.P.G. and Ruiter, M.L. (2005), *Determinanten van deprivate R&D-uitgaven in internationaal perspectief [Determinants of the private R&D intensity in an international perspective]*, Ministry of Economic Affairs and Dialogic, The Hague.

Gallouj, F. (2002), *Innovation in the Service Economy: the New Wealth of Nations*, Cheltenham, Edward Elgar.

Gallouj, F. and O. Weinstein (1997), *Innovation in services*, Research Policy, 26, pp. 537-556.

Hollanders, H. and Arundel, A (2004), "2004 European Innovation Scoreboard Methodology Report, European Trend Chart on Innovation, A discussion paper from the Innovation/SMEs Programme", *www.trendchart.org/scoreboards/scoreboard2004/scoreboard_papers.cfm*, Item 10, accessed July 2005.

Innovation Platform (2003), *Grenzeloze Mobiliteit Kennismigranten: Hoe krijgen we het talent naar Nederland toe?* [*Borderless Mobility of Knowledge Migrants: How to get talent towards the Netherlands?*, only in Dutch], The Hague.

MERIT (2003), *Brain Drain – Emigration Flows for Qualified Scientists*, project for the European Commission, Maastricht.

Messina, Juliàn (2004), *Institutions and service employment: A panel study for OECD countries*, ECB Working Paper, nr. 320.

Ministry of Economic Affairs (2004), *Visie op het vestigingsklimaat door in Nederland gevestigde buitenlandse bedrijven* [Vision on the location climate of foreign companies located in the Netherlands], The Hague.

Ministry of Economic Affairs (2005), *Strong basis for delivering top performance – Renewed instruments for entrepreneurs from the Ministry of Economic Affairs*, The Hague.

Ministry of Economic Affairs and Ministry of Education, Culture and Science (2004), *Science, Technology and Innovation in the Netherlands: Policies, facts and figures*, The Hague.

Ministry of Economic Affairs and Ministry of Social Affairs and Employment (2004), Agenda for Growth: Prosperity now and later, The Hague.

Ministry of Finance (2002), *Samenwerken en Stroomlijnen: Opties voor een effectief innovatiebeleid* (eindrapportage IBO technologiebeleid) [*co-operation and simplification: Options for an effective innovation policy*, Dutch only], The Hague.

Ministry of Education, Culture and Sciences (2003), *Wetenschapsbudget 2004: focus op excellentie en meer waarde* [*Sciences Budget 2004: focus on excellence and value added*, Dutch only], The Hague.

Ministry of Education, Culture and Science (2004), *Financiering in het hoger onderwijs: meer flexibiliteit, meer keuzevrijheid, meer kwaliteit* [Financing higher education: more flexibility, more choices, more quality, Dutch only], policy note, The Hague.

Ministry of Education, Culture and Science (2005), *Experimenten met een open bestel in het hoger onderwijs* [*Experimenting with removing barriers to entry to the publicly funded market of higher education*, Dutch only], policy note, The Hague.

Nicoletti, G., S. Golub, D. Hajkova, D. Mirza and K.Y. Yoo (2003) Policies and International Integration: Influences on Trade and Foreign Direct Investment, OECD Economics Department Working Papers, No. 359.

OECD (2003b), *The Sources of Economic Growth in OECD Countries*, Paris.

OECD (2004), *Public-Private Partnerships for Research and Innovation. The Dutch Experience*, OECD, Paris.

OECD (2005a), *Science, Technology and Industry Scoreboard*, OECD, Paris.

OECD (2005b), *Main Science and Technology Indicators*, 2005:1, Paris.

OECD (2005e), *Education at a Glance, OECD indicators 2005*, Paris.

OECD (2005c), *OECD Economic Outlook 78 database*, Paris.

OECD (2005d), *OECD Factbook: Economics, Environmental and Social Statistics*, Paris.

OECD (2005f), *SME and Entrepreneurship Outlook – 2005 Edition*, OECD, Paris.

Pain, N. and Jaumotte, F. (2005), "Innovation in the business sector", *OECD Economics Department Working Papers*, No. 459, forthcoming.

Platform Anders Betalen voor Mobiliteit (2005), *Advies Nationaal Platform Anders Betalen voor Mobiliteit* [Advice of the National Platform Paying for Mobility in a Different Way], The Hague.

Scarpetta, S., Hemmings, P. Tressel, T. and Woo, J (2002), The Role of Policy and Institutions for Productivity and Firm Dynamics: Evidence form Micro and Industry Data, ECO/WKP(2002)15, Paris.

UNCTAD (2004), World investment report 2004: The shift towards services, Switzerland.

ANNEX 5.A1

Factor analysis to identify inter-related
EIS innovation indicators

Introduction

While the indicators included in the European Innovation Scoreboard (EIS) Summary Index (European Commission, 2004a) are all in some way *a priori* related to innovation activity, it will help to focus the analysis in Chapter 5 by empirically determining which of these variables are in fact related to the same underlying phenomena and setting aside the other variables. The factor analysis that underpins the groups of inter-related variables selected for further analysis in chapter 5 is described in this annex.

Factor analysis to identify inter-related variables and exclude others

Factor analysis[1] based on 20 EIS indicators (Table 5A.1)[2] for the OECD 20 countries[3] shows that 45% of the common variance shared by the 20 variables can be explained by the first factor (Table 5A.2, "proportion" column). A further 21% of the common variance is explained by the second factor, bringing the cumulative proportion of the common variance explained to 66%. As subsequent factors add relatively little to explaining the common variance, they are set aside.

Ten of the innovation indicators load onto Factor 1 with a cut-off value for the correlation between the indicator and this factor of 0.7 (Table 5.A1.3, identifies these variables with a * in the Factor 1 column). Considering the nature of the variables, they appear to reflect "*knowledge development*". Four other innovation indicators load onto Factor 2 (see Table 5.A1.3, variables identified with a * in the Factor 2 column). These indicators mostly appear to reflect "*knowledge application*".

On average the Netherlands ranks 9th out of the OECD 20 countries for the indicators of "knowledge development" (Table 5.A1.4); lowest ranks for individual indicators range from 16-20 depending on available data. The Netherlands does particularly well on EPO high-tech patent applications (Item 2.3.1) and public R&D expenditure as a share of GDP (Item 2.1) but scores below average on the proportion of the population with tertiary education (Item 1.2) and business expenditures on R&D as a percentage of GDP (Item 2.2); the Netherlands ranks around the middle of the group for the other indicators. The Netherlands does not score very well on the "knowledge application" indicators, ranking 14th equal out of 17 high-income countries for which data are available (EU15 less Ireland plus Switzerland, Norway and Iceland) (Table 5.A1.5). It scores relatively poorly on all four indicators loaded to this factor, with especially low rankings for the percentage of SMEs

Table 5.A1.1. **Innovation item classification and source of data**[1]

Innovation item	Source of data
1. Human resources	
1.1. S&E graduates ([permil] of 20 – 29 years age class)	EUROSTAT (Education statistics)
1.2. Population with tertiary education (% of 25 – 64 years age class)	EUROSTAT (LFS)
1.3. Participation in life-long learning (% of 25 – 64 years age class)	EUROSTAT (LFS)
1.4. Employment in medium-high and high-tech manufacturing (% of total workforce)	EUROSTAT (LFS)
1.5. Employment in high-tech services (% of total workforce)	EUROSTAT (LFS)
2. Knowledge creation	
2.1. Public R&D expenditures (% of GDP)	EUROSTAT (R&D statistics); OECD
2.2. Business expenditures on R&D (% of GDP)	EUROSTAT (R&D statistics); OECD
2.3.1. EPO high-tech patent applications (per million population)	EUROSTAT
2.3.2. USPTO high-tech patents granted (per million population)	EUROSTAT
2.4.1. EPO patent applications (per million population)	EUROSTAT
2.4.2. USPTO patents granted (per million population)	EUROSTAT
3. Transmission and application of knowledge	
3.1. SMEs innovating in-house (% of all SMEs)	EUROSTAT (CIS)
3.2. SMEs involved in innovation co-operation (% of all SMEs)	EUROSTAT (CIS)
3.3. Innovation expenditures (% of total turnover)	EUROSTAT (CIS)
3.4. SMEs using non-technological change (% of all SMEs)	EUROSTAT (CIS)
4. Innovation finance, output and markets	
4.1. Share of high-tech venture capital investment	EVCA
4.2. Share of early stage venture capital in GDP	EUROSTAT
4.3.1. Sales of "new to market' products (% of total turnover)	EUROSTAT (CIS)
4.3.2. Sales of "new to the firm but not new to the market' products (% of total turnover)	EUROSTAT (CIS)
4.4. Internet access	EUROSTAT
4.5. ICT expenditures (% of GDP)	EUROSTAT
4.6. Share of manufacturing value-added in high-tech sectors	EUROSTAT (SBS)

1. *www.trendchart.org/scoreboards/scoreboard2004/indicators.cfm*, accessed August 2005.

Source: Trend Chart Innovation Policy in Europe (*www.trendchart.org/scoreboards/scoreboard2004/indicators.cfm*). Detailed descriptions of the indicators can be found in Hollanders and Arundel (2004).

Table 5.A1.2. **Factor analysis results: 20 items**

Factor	Eigenvalue[1]	Difference[2]	Proportion	Cumulative proportion
1	8.94	4.72	0.45	0.45
2	4.22	2.13	0.21	0.66
3	2.09	0.42	0.10	0.76
4	1.68	0.52	0.08	0.85
5	1.16	0.25	0.06	0.90
6	0.91	0.48	0.05	0.95
7	0.44	0.13	0.02	0.97
8	0.31	0.06	0.02	0.99
9	0.25	0.25	0.01	1.00

1. Eigenvalue: an eigenvalue is the variance in a set of variables explained by a factor. In the initial factor solution, the first factor will account for the most variance, the second will account for the next highest amount of variance, and so on.
2. Difference: Gives the differences between the current and previous eigenvalues.

Source: European Commission (2004b), European Innovation Scoreboard 2004 database; own calculations.

using non-technological change (Item 3.4) and for total innovation expenditures as a share of turnover (Item 3.3); the other two indicators with low rankings are the proportion of SMEs innovating in-house (Item 3.1) and sales of products that are new to the firm but not the market as a percentage of total turnover (Item 4.3.2).

Table 5.A1.3. **Factor loadings**

Item	Loading	Factor 1	Loading	Factor 2
1.1. S&E graduates ([permil] of 20 – 29 years age class)	0.53		0.06	
1.2. Population with tertiary education (% of 25 – 64 years age class)	0.78	*	−0.29	
1.3. Participation in life-long learning (% of 25 – 64 years age class)	0.73	*	−0.56	
1.4. Employment in medium-high and high-tech manufacturing (% of total workforce)	0.19		0.64	
1.5. Employment in high-tech services (% of total workforce)	0.88	*	−0.17	
2.1. Public R&D expenditures (% of GDP)	0.89	*	0.19	
2.2. Business expenditures on R&D (% of GDP)	0.90	*	0.29	
2.3.1. EPO high-tech patent applications (per million population)	0.85	*	0.19	
2.3.2. USPTO high-tech patents granted (per million population)	0.87	*	0.35	
3.1. SMEs innovating in-house (% of all SMEs)	−0.02		0.80	*
3.2. SMEs involved in innovation co-operation (% of all SMEs)	0.95	*	−0.04	
3.3. Innovation expenditures (% of total turnover)	−0.07		0.82	*
3.4. SMEs using non-technological change (% of all SMEs)	−0.33		0.74	*
4.1. Share of high-tech venture capital investment	0.35		0.25	
4.2. Share of early stage venture capital in GDP	0.89	*	−0.13	
4.3.1. Sales of "new to market' products (% of total turnover)	0.12		0.57	
4.3.2. Sales of "new to the firm but not new to the market' products (% of total turnover)	−0.07		0.86	*
4.4. Internet access	0.68		−0.21	
4.5. ICT expenditures (% of GDP)	0.63		0.08	
4.6. Share of manufacturing value-added in high-tech sectors	0.89	*	0.22	

Source: European Commission (2004b), European Innovation Scoreboard 2004 database; own calculations.

Table 5.A1.4. **Rankings of OECD 20 countries for innovation items that load on "Knowledge Development"**

	Rank Item 1.2	Rank Item 1.3	Rank Item 1.5	Rank Item 2.1	Rank Item 2.2	Rank Item 2.3.1	Rank Item 2.3.2	Rank Item 3.2	Rank Item 4.2	Rank Item 4.6	Factor 1 Item average rank
Finland	3	7	3	2	2	1	3	1	2	3	2.7
Sweden	8	1	1	3	1	3	4	3	1	8	3.3
USA	1	n.a.	n.a.	4	5	5	1	n.a.	4	4	3.4
Japan	2	n.a.	n.a.	7	3	9	2	n.a.	n.a.	7	5.0
Iceland	10	3	2	1	6	8	5	5	7	n.a.	5.2
Switzerland	9	2	7	11	4	4	6	6	5	1	5.5
Denmark	4	6	4	8	7	7	7	2	3	9	5.7
UK	6	5	5	13	12	10	10	12	6	5	8.4
Netherlands	12	8	11	6	14	2	9	8	11	11	9.2
France	15	12	6	5	11	11	11	9	9	6	9.5
Belgium	7	10	8	15	9	12	12	7	10	10	10.0
Norway	5	4	10	10	15	15	15	4	8	14	10.0
Germany	14	14	13	9	8	6	8	10	14	12	10.8
Ireland	11	9	9	19	16	13	13	n.a.	13	2	11.7
Austria	17	11	12	12	13	14	14	11	15	13	13.2
Luxembourg	18	13	14	20	10	16	18	n.a.	n.a.	19	16.0
Spain	13	15	16	17	17	18	17	16	16	16	16.1
Italy	20	16	15	16	18	17	16	15	18	15	16.6
Portugal	19	18	18	14	19	20	20	13	12	17	17.0
Greece	16	17	17	18	20	19	19	14	17	18	17.5

Source: European Commission (2004b), European Innovation Scoreboard 2004 database; own calculations.

Table 5.A1.5. **Rankings of OECD 20 countries for innovation items that load on "Knowledge Application"**

	Rank Item 3.1	Rank Item 3.3	Rank Item 3.4	Rank Item 4.3.2	Factor 2 item average rank
Switzerland	1	1	n.a.	2	1.3
Germany	3	2	2	1	2.0
Belgium	5	3	7	8	5.8
Finland	6	6	9	3	6.0
Portugal	7	4	6	7	6.0
Austria	8	n.a.	4	10	7.3
Luxembourg	4	12	1	14	7.8
Italy	11	8	8	5	8.0
Iceland	2	10	5	16	8.3
Greece	16	7	3	13	9.8
Sweden	9	n.a.	11	n.a.	10.0
United Kingdom	15	9	n.a.	6	10.0
Spain	14	13	10	4	10.3
France	12	5	15	12	11.0
Netherlands	10	11	12	11	11.0
Denmark	17	15	14	9	13.8
Norway	13	14	13	15	13.8
Ireland	n.a.	n.a.	n.a.	n.a.	n.a.
Japan	n.a.	n.a.	n.a.	n.a.	n.a.
United States	n.a.	n.a.	n.a.	n.a.	n.a.

Source: European Commission (2004b), European Innovation Scoreboard 2004 database; own calculations.

Notes

1. "(Factor analysis aims) to explain the variability among a number of observable random variables in terms of a smaller number of unobservable random variables called factors. The observed random variables are modelled as linear combinations of the factors, plus 'error' terms. The factor loadings (are) inferred from the data." *http://en.wikipedia.org/wiki/Factor_analysis.*

2. Indicators 2.4.1 (EPO patent applications (per million population)) and 2.4.2 (USPTO patents granted (per million population)) have been excluded because they are highly related to indicators 2.3.1 (EPO high-tech patent applications (per million population)) and 2.3.2 (USPTO high-tech patents granted (per million population)), respectively.

3. As this procedure employs casewise deletion, meaning that information from countries with at least one missing value from the selected variables is excluded prior to performing the calculation, the EIS dataset is cut down to the OECD 20 group of countries: EU15, Iceland, Japan, Norway, Switzerland, and the United States.

Bibliography

European Commission, "EUROPA, A new start for the Lisbon Strategy", *http://europa.eu.int/growthandjobs/index_en.htm*, accessed September, 2005.

European Commission (2004a), "European Innovation Scoreboard 2004: Comparative analysis of innovation performance", Commission Staff Working Paper, Brussels, 19.11.2004 SEC(2004) 1475, *www.trendchart.org/scoreboards/scoreboard2004/scoreboard_papers.cfm*, accessed July 2005.

European Commission (2004b), European Innovation Scoreboard 2004 Database, *www.trendchart.org/scoreboards/scoreboard2004/pdf/eis_2004_database.xls*

Hollanders, H. and Arundel, A (2004), "2004 European Innovation Scoreboard Methodology Report, European Trend Chart on Innovation, A discussion paper from the Innovation/SMEs Programme", *www.trendchart.org/scoreboards/scoreboard2004/scoreboard_papers.cfm*, Item 10, accessed July 2005.

Glossary of Acronyms

ADV	Shortening of work time (*Arbeidsuur verkorting*)
ASPASIA	Programme to increase the number of women senior lecturers
AWBZ	Long-term Health Care Insurance Act (*Algemene Wet Bijzondere Ziektekosten*)
CBS	National Statistics Office (*Centraal Bureau voor de Statistiek*)
CINOP	Centre for the Innovation of Education and Training
CHEPS	Centre for Higher Education Policy Studies
CPB	Netherlands Bureau for Economic Policy Analysis (*Centraal Planbureau*)
CWI	Centre for Works and Income (*Centrum voor Werk en Inkomen*)
DB	Disability Benefit
DNB	Dutch Central Bank (*De Nederlandsche Bank*)
DPI	Dutch Polymer Institute
EATR	Effective Average Tax Rate
ECN	Energy Research Centre of the Netherlands
EIS	European Innovation Scoreboard
EET	Exempt-Exempt-Tax
EPL	Employment Projection Legislation
EPO	European Patent Office
EU15	European Union, 15 Member States
E&Y	Ernst and Young
EVC	Experience and Skill Certification
EVD	Agency for International Business and Cooperation
FDI	Foreign Direct Investment
FES	Fund for Strengthening the Economic Structure
FNV	Trade Union Confederation
FSAP	Financial Services Action Plan
GDP	Gross Domestic Product
GeoDelft	National Institute/or Geo-Engineering
GTI	Large technological institute (*Grote Technologische Institute*)
HBO-WO	Higher vocational education (*Hoger Beroepsonderwijs*)
HRST	Human Resources in Science and Technology
ICT	Information and Communication Technology
IP	Innovation Platform
IPR	Intellectual Property Rights
KNAW	Royal Netherlands Academy of Arts and Sciences
KPN	Royal Dutch Telecom
MARIN	Maritime Research Institute in the Netherlands

MEA	Ministry of Economic Affaires
MECS	Ministry of Education, Culture and Science
MINAS	Minimum Accounting System
NAIRU	Non-accelerating inflation rate of unemployment
NIMR	Netherlands Institute for Metals Research
NLR	National Aerospace Laboratory
NMa	Dutch Competition Agency (*Nederlandse Mededingingsagentschap*)
NS	Dutch railways (*Nederlandse Spoorwegen*)
NWO	Netherlands Organisation for Scientific Research
NZa	Dutch Healthcare Authority (*Nederlands Zorg autoriteit*)
PDV/GDV	Zoning policy on peripheral and large scale retail outlets
PEMBA	Experience rating of disability insurance premiums
PMR	Product Market Regulation
PRO	Public Research Organisations
R&D	Research and Development
S&E	Science and Engineering
SBIR	Small Business Innovation and Research Initiative
SenterNovem	Agency of the MEA for implementing innovation and sustainable development policies
SER	Social and Economic Council (*Sociaal-Economische Raad*)
SKE	Technopartner Knowledge Exploitation Subsidy Arrangement
SMEs	Small and Medium-sized Enterprises
TNO	Netherlands Organisation for Applied Scientific Research
TPG	Royal TPG Post
TTI	Top Technological Institutes (*Technologische Top Instituten*)
TTO	Technological Transfer Organisations
UB	Unemployment benefit
UWV	UB and DB agency (*Uitvoeringsinstituut Werknemersverzekering*)
WAO	Disability Insurance Act (*Wet op de Arbeidsongeschiktheidsverzekering*)
WBSO	Fiscal stimulation for research and development (*Fiscale Stimulering voor Speur en Ontwikkelingswerk*)
WCFS	Wageningen Centre for Food Sciences
WL/Delft Hydraulics	Research Centre for Water management and Engineering

OECD PUBLICATIONS, 2, rue André-Pascal, 75775 PARIS CEDEX 16
PRINTED IN FRANCE
(10 2006 02 1 P) ISBN 92-64-03669-5 – No. 54961 2006